D0407695

Kite Making and Flying

HAROLD RIDGWAY

Kite Making and Flying

GRAMERCY PUBLISHING COMPANY • NEW YORK

PRINTED IN THE UNITED STATES OF AMERICA

This edition published by Gramercy Publishing Company,
a division of Crown Publishers, Inc.,
by arrangement with MacGibbon & Kee, Ltd. (Arco)

I

Contents

Preface

WHEN it was first suggested that my husband should write a book about Kite Making and Flying, I must confess that I, like the rest of my family, was very surprised. I wondered what there would be to write about. After all, making and flying a kite are quite simple operations! One has only to tie together two sticks at right angles, cover them with paper or cloth, and add a tail! Of course, one must not forget a long piece of string, called the kite line. Having done these things, one has only to throw the kite up into the air on a suitably windy day and away it flies! Or—does it?

My husband hastily assured me that there was much more to the business than this, and, as he began to explain to me some of the technicalities of the subject, I realized that he knew far more about it than I had suspected.

Since that time, there have been visits to libraries and business premises; letters to individuals and firms; the house has been filled with specimens of cane, string, cloth and paper; models of kites have been looking down at us from their places on the walls; discussions about weather conditions and the science of flight have taken place, and a whole new world seems to have opened before my eyes.

Here, then, is a hobby which provides pleasure, entertainment, and education all the year round. The long winter evenings present an opportunity for artistic minds and busy hands to make the kites which can be flown during the bright summer evenings and at many other times during the year. These are the main things, but, as we shall discover, they are accompanied by many other enjoyable activities. In particular, as one looks round in an attempt to forecast flying conditions, one is reminded of the wonder and the beauty of the world in which we live.

My heart leaps up when I behold
A rainbow in the sky

7

So wrote the poet, Wordsworth, and something of that same feeling will come over us as we see our kites—those kites which we have made with our own hands—flying so proudly in the sky above.

PHYLLIS RIDGWAY

A word in general

IN the first section of the book (Chapters 1–8) instructions and diagrams are given for making 19 different kites. It will be found that some are easy to make; others require more time and skill. Again, there are several sizes which range, for example, from the 'Small Fish' kite to the large Box kite.

This selection is offered for certain reasons. One is to help the beginner to progress from the simpler to the more complex forms. In this way he will gain skill in making and handling many different kites, and at the same time he may build up a collection of which he can be justly proud.

Another and related reason is that many people do not know how large the scope is in kite design. These chapters will reveal something of that scope, and so may serve to correct the idea that kites are limited to the Box and Pegtop styles. Literally speaking, dozens of different styles could be made, and they would fly, if certain rules were kept. From the large number available, a selection has been made in which the reader may find much that is of interest and satisfaction to him.

The rest of the book (Chapters 9–13) is concerned with a number of important things, each of which forms a part of kite-craft. They may serve to prove that this hobby opens a door to a variety of interesting activities and studies. The writer's intention has been to present in as simple a way as is possible the obvious and less obvious factors in kite making and flying. It is earnestly hoped that the book may succeed in attracting many new friends to a hobby which can be of absorbing interest to all who take it up.

PART ONE

Kites to Make: Making: Flying

CHAPTER ONE

Tonking: Pegtop: Loose Cover

THE TONKING KITE

As its name implies, this kite is of eastern origin. It has a very simple structure, about which brief comment may be made. First, it is light in weight, because there is a broad wing or cover area with a minimum of framework. This is known as low wing loading, and it is important if the kite is to be successful in flight. Secondly, the kite is bow shaped. This upward inclination of the wing is known as positive dihedral. It improves stability; and in the third place, this stability is further aided by the use of a two-piece bridle, which provides side-to-side balance. Fourthly, the extended backbone permits the effective bracing of the framework.

The framework is formed by three strips, comprising a backbone, A, and two crossbars, B and C (Fig. 1). The backbone is 2 ft. in length and is cut from $\frac{1}{4}$ in. square hard stripwood. It is notched at the ends in the manner shown at D (Fig. 1). This piece should be straight and smooth and free from knots or splits. The crossbars are each 2 ft. in length, and are made from split cane, about $\frac{1}{4}$ in. thick. Failing this, $\frac{1}{4}$ in. square stripwood may be used, though it is not so strong or flexible as cane. The crossbars are also notched at the ends (E, Fig. 1). These notches are for the bracing strings, which are added later.

The crossbars are now shaped to a curve. The method of doing this is described in Chapter 7 under the heading 'Shaping Wood and Cane'. The depth of the curve at the centre is 2 in., and the crossbars are held in shape by bowstrings, after the manner of making a bow for archery. The bowstrings should be taut, otherwise the crossbars may spring out of shape.

Secure the crossbars to the backbone, 3 in. from each end. The bowstrings lie clear of the framework on the underside. Use glue and strong thread to make the joints, and make sure that these are really firm and do not move from side to side.

The framework is braced with thin strong string. See the notes on string for kites in Chapter 7 under the heading 'Materials'. Begin by tying the string to the top of the backbone, and pass it

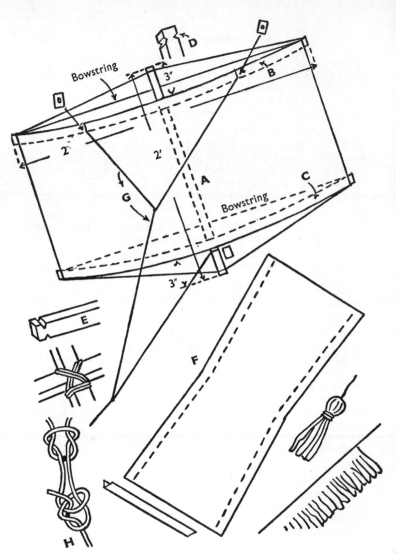

FIG. 1. Tonking

in turn round the ends of the framework. Bring it back to the top
of the backbone, and tie securely. There should be an even tension
on the string, but do not bend any part of the framework to
secure this. The backbone must be straight and the crossbars
parallel to each other, if the kite is to fly successfully.

Now cover the framework with paper. Tissue paper, pure
unbleached greaseproof or pure ribbed kraft may be used. See
the notes on paper in Chapter 7, under the heading 'Materials'.
Cut the paper to the required shape (F, Fig. 1) this allows a 2 in.
margin at the top and bottom for overlapping the crossbars. Cut
narrow V-shaped slits at regular intervals along the margins.
The cover may now be decorated. Suggested designs are given in
Chapter 7, in the section on 'Accessories'.

The cover is secured to the framework with thin glue, the
margins overlapping the crossbars. It will be seen that the cover
is not an exact oblong, being wider at the ends than in the middle.
This means that when it is fixed in place, the middle area will be
tightly stretched, and the ends will be rather loose by comparison.
This slackness should be equal at both ends. Take care not to
wrinkle the paper. Paper strips, 4 in. in width, are glued over the
crossbars and the short sides of the cover, for strengthening.

The bridle (G, Fig. 1) is formed in two parts. The string for the
top loop is 2 ft. 6 in. in length. It is tied to the top crossbar, 6 in.
from each end. The bottom loop requires a 3 ft. 6 in. length of
string. This is tied at the centre of the top loop, and also to the
backbone just below the bottom joint. Glue a small block of $\frac{1}{4}$ in.
stripwood to the backbone, just below this tying point to prevent
the bridle from slipping. It will be realized that the cover will
have to be pierced when the top loop is being tied. Glue thin
cardboard washers to the cover at these places to prevent the
paper from tearing in flight.

The kite line is attached to the bridle by means of a bowline
knot and a reef knot. See H (Fig. 1) for an illustration of these.
Further notes on knots will be found in Chapter 7, under the
heading 'Methods'. These knots will permit the line to be adjusted
on the bridle, so as to obtain the best angle for flying the kite. A
kite flies at an angle to the wind and the most effective one is
found by experiment.

A few optional extras will enhance the appearance of the kite.
For example, fringes may be fastened to the top and bottom

bracing strings, and a tassel suspended from the bottom of the backbone. Such extras are described in Chapter 7, under the heading 'Accessories'.

THE PEGTOP KITE

The Pegtop is a good choice if one is looking for an easy-to-make kite. The framework is a simple two-piece unit. When this is covered, and a bridle and tail added, the kite is ready for flying. It is not, however, one of the easiest of kites to handle. Technically, this is because it lacks inherent stability. Stability means that if a kite is disturbed from its path of steady flight by, say, a change of wind direction or speed, it will tend to right itself. Inherent stability means that this balance or steadiness is achieved by the design and construction of the kite. We may say then that the pegtop kite tends to be unstable in a changeable wind. This very fact, however, may be an additional reason for making such a kite, and the operator finds much satisfaction in skilfully handling it in flight.

The pegtop may be made in different sizes. The measurements given here could be adapted to suit individual requirements. It must be remembered, though, that the larger the kite, the more skill is needed in flying it successfully. The one described here may be thought of as a small trial size, which will teach the young beginner quite a lot about the art of flying kites.

The backbone A (Fig. 2) is formed from $\frac{1}{4}$ in. $\times$ $\frac{3}{8}$ in. stripwood, 1 ft. 6 in. in length and is notched at the bottom end. It must be straight and smooth. For the curved top use a flexible piece of split cane about $\frac{1}{4}$ in. diameter and 1 ft. 4 in. in length, and notch it at the ends. Suitable cane may be obtained from handicraft or horticultural shops. That which has a hard outer skin is the kind which is the best to use. It may be bought in 3 ft. lengths. If they are whole pieces, they can be split with a sharp-pointed knife.

The cane is curved to a bow shape, as shown (B, Fig. 2). The shaping is more easily done if the cane is subjected to dry heat, such as a gas jet or electric fire. This prevents cracking or splitting. The bow is held in position by means of a bowstring, C, tied at each end. Use thin, strong string because it has to withstand considerable strain. The depth of the curve at the centre is $3\frac{1}{2}$ in.

Secure the cane at its centre to the top of the backbone. Use

glue and bind round with strong thread. Apply glue to the binding to prevent it from slipping. Make a neat, firm joint. The
strength of the framework depends upon this.

The next stage is to complete the bracing of the framework.
Use thin strong string. Tie this to one end of the curved top. From
there take it to the bottom of the backbone and up to the other

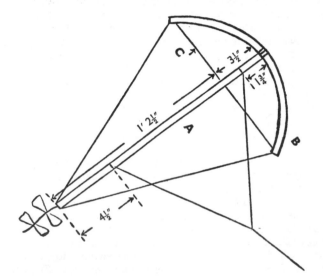

FIG. 2. Pegtop

end of the top. This string should not be too taut, as most of the
strain is taken up by the bowstring. The framework is now complete, and is ready for covering.

For the cover use tissue paper or pure unbleached greaseproof.
(It is worth while mentioning here, that a larger size in this kind
of kite, say 3 ft. or over, would be better with a lightweight cloth
cover.) Place the framework on the paper and with a pencil mark
out the shape of the cover. Allow a margin of 1½ in. all round and
cut out. At this point the cover may be decorated. Suggested

designs are given in 'Accessories' in Chapter 7. These are best done on separate sheets of paper and pasted on to the cover. For colouring, one of the proprietary brands of lacquer is easy to apply, and will answer the purpose well.

Attach the cover to the framework, taking care not to crease or tear the paper. Apply glue to the backbone, and stick the cover to it and set aside for a little while for the glue to dry. Next, cut narrow V-shaped slits at intervals round the margin. Apply glue to the curved top, and to the outer half of the margin. Fold this over and fasten it down around the top and the outer strings. 3 in. folded reinforcing strips may be glued round the strings and the top.

The kite may be embellished with tassels or fringes. If fringes are chosen, then two loops of string are tied to the ends of the bow and the bottom of the backbone. If tassels are chosen, they would hang from the ends of the curved top. Details for making both of these are given in 'Accessories'.

The bridle, 3 ft. 6 in. in length, is tied to the backbone at the places shown (Fig. 2) in the form of a loop. Use stout string. In order to attach the bridle, the cover has to be pierced. Strengthen the cover where this is done by means of thin cardboard washers, fastened down with glue.

A conventional tail is tied to the bottom of the backbone. This is a piece of string 4 ft. 6 in. in length to which are fastened 4 in. folded strips of paper 6 in. apart. (See 'Accessories' for further details.) For the kite line use the kind recommended in Chapter 7. It is attached to the bridle by means of a bowline knot and a reef knot. The method of forming the knots is shown in Chapter 7. These permit the line to be adjusted on the bridle, in order to obtain the best position for flying the kite. Generally the kite line is tied a little above the centre of gravity. This centre may be ascertained by balancing the kite by its backbone on a length of thin stripwood, or even the blunt end of a pencil would serve. The point when the kite remains in balance on the stick is the centre of gravity, and this could be marked with a pencil.

A reel is needed on which the kite string is wound. Two types of these are described in 'Accessories'. The size of the reel will depend to a large extent upon the amount and thickness of the string used, but both of the reels referred to are of a convenient size.

Loose Cover Kite

This kite flies on a different principle from most kites. In action it is more like the sail of a boat which billows out in the wind. In effect the action of the sail forms what may be called an anhedral angle, which is reverse in shape to dihedral.

It is a tail-less type, and lacking the measure of steadiness which a tail provides, it can be rather erratic in flight. Nevertheless, its lively manner makes it an interesting kite to fly.

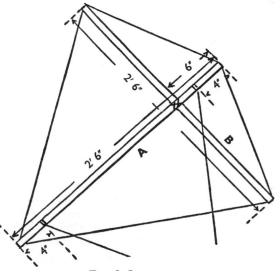

FIG. 3. Loose cover

The framework is of the simplest kind, comprising a backbone and cross-strut (A and B, Fig. 3) which are arranged in the form of a cross. The kite can be made so that the framework will fold up for convenience in transport. Two pieces of ⅜ in. square strip-wood are required. These are 2 ft. 6 in. in length. Notch these pieces at the ends and lash them together with fine string, the cross-strut being 6 in. from the top of the backbone. As this kite may be folded up when required, no glue is used in making the framework joint. Tie the binding string in such a manner that it may readily be removed.

The bracing string is fitted next. Use thin, strong string and take it over the ends of the framework by means of the notches provided. Tie the ends at the bottom of the backbone.

The cover is made of lightweight cotton material, such as cambric. It is cut rather wider than the frame, so that it bellies out like a sail in the wind. Lay the framework on the material with an extra 2½ in. all round, 1 in. of which forms the overlap, and cut out. When decorating the cover, mark out the design in pencil and colour it with fabric painting oil colours. A simple bold design is most effective, and bright colours should be used. Note that the design is painted on the front side, where the bridle is tied (Fig. 3).

To attach the cover, sew the 1 in. margin neatly down over the bracing string, but do not fasten it to the framework. In this way the cross-strut may be removed, laid along the backbone, and the cover wrapped round them when the kite is being taken from place to place.

The bridle is formed of strong string which is 5 ft. in length. It is tied in a loop, 4 in. from each end of the backbone. The kite line is attached to the bridle with a bowline knot and a reef knot so that the upper part of the bridle is shorter than the lower part. The exact tying point will be found by experiment, and adjustments to secure this are easily made.

Though this kite does not usually have a tail, it may be a help to fit a short one if the kite behaves too erratically in flight.

CHAPTER TWO

High Flyer No. 1:
High Flyer No. 2: Hexagonal

HIGH FLYER KITE NO. 1

THERE are very good reports of the flying performance of this kite. It will readily attain a good height, and being strongly made will withstand fairly rough weather. The framework is constructed of split cane throughout to give maximum strength, and the two-piece bridle and tail improve stability.

To make the kite you will require three pieces of split cane, A, B, and C, all about $\frac{1}{4}$ in. thick. The backbone A, is 2 ft. 6 in. in length, and the crossbars, B and C, are each 2 ft. Make shallow grooves at the end of all three pieces, and assemble them in the pattern shown in Fig. 4. The angles between the framework pieces must correspond on each side of the backbone, otherwise the kite will not balance well. Join the framework pieces together with glue and fine string. The joint thus made comes at the centre of the backbone and crossbars. Make sure that this joint is strongly made, otherwise the framework will be in danger of collapsing when the kite is in flight.

The bracing strings are added next. Begin with the inner one. Take a length of thin strong string, and tie it to the top half of the backbone, exactly half way between the end and the centre joint. From there, take it to one of the crossbars, at a point which is half way between one end and the centre joint. Bind the string round the crossbar once or twice and tie with an overhand knot. Smear the binding with glue to prevent it slipping. Repeat the procedure until the inner bracing is completed. Add the outer bracing string in the same way, making use of the grooves which have been cut at the ends of the framework. The bracing strings should be taut, in order to keep the kite in its proper shape.

The cover is made from lightweight cotton material, such as cambric, or very fine calico. Lay the framework on the material, mark the shape with a pencil, allowing an extra 1 in. all round for overlapping, and cut out. Paint a simple design in bright colours on the cover, using fabric painting oil colours. Pin the cover to a board while this is being done.

Now attach the cover to the outer bracing strings. Fold the margin over these and stitch it neatly in place. Try to get an even tension on the cover, which should also be smooth and free from wrinkles.

The next thing to do is to add the bridle strings. Take a piece

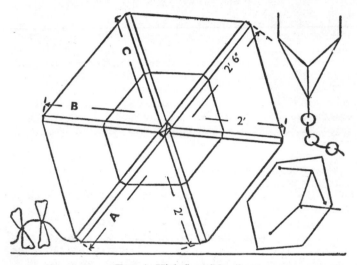

Fig. 4. High flyer (No. 1)

of strong string, which is 3 ft. in length and tie it at a point which is 6 in. from the bottom of the backbone. Pierce the cover here, and thread the string through. A second piece of string, which is 4 ft. 6 in. in length is tied in the form of a loop to the top ends of the crossbars. Tie the bottom string to the centre of the loop and the bridle is complete. Attach the kite line to the bottom bridle string by means of a reef knot and a bowline knot, which will permit the line to be adjusted in order to obtain the best angle for flying the kite. See Chapter 7 on knots, under the heading 'Methods'.

The tail is formed by three pieces of fine string. Two pieces, each 2 ft. in length, are tied to the bottom ends of the crossbars. The third piece, which is 5 ft. in length, is tied to the bottom of the backbone. Lay the kite on a table, pull the bottom tail string tight and tie the other two strings to it, so that they too are taut. Thread a number of thin cardboard discs on to the tail string, by means of four holes punched in the discs. Make these discs in different colours, or glue metallic foil paper to them so that they will glitter in the light. Position them about 6 in. apart on the line and tie the latter in a bow at the end.

If desired, a pennant may be flown from the top of the back-bone. See 'Accessories' in Chapter 7 for making these. Altogether this is a strong and attractive kite, with a good performance. An alternative conventional tail is shown in the illustration.

HIGH FLYER NO. 2

Here is another easily made kite with a good flying performance. Like the High Flyer No. 1 the framework is formed of split cane, about $\frac{1}{4}$ in. thick, because of its lightness and strength.

First cut the horizontal bar, A, which is 2 ft. in length, and the crossbars, B and C, which are each 2 ft. 8 in. in length. Make shallow grooves at the ends of these pieces, and assemble them, following the pattern shown in Fig. 5. Note that the bottom ends of C and B are in a straight line with the ends of A. Make the joint secure with glue and bind round with thin string.

Next, add the bracing string which should be fine and strong. Tie a length of this to the end of one of the framework pieces and then take the string round to form an outline, making use of the grooves provided. The string should be taut and firmly tied.

The cover is made from cambric or very fine calico. Lay the framework on the material and mark out the shape, allowing an extra 1 in. all round for overlapping. The marking is made easier if the material is first pinned to a board, and whilst it is pinned, it may also be decorated, if desired. Choose a simple design and execute it in bright colours, using fabric painting oil colours. Allow sufficient time for the colours to dry.

Now attach the cover to the bracing string. Fold the margin over this and sew it down. The cover should be as smooth and firm as possible. Glue strips of cloth to the cover and over the

ends of the framework pieces B and C, thus providing extra
security for the cover.

The bridle is formed in the manner shown (Fig. 5), and tied
at the places marked with an X. A piece of strong string, 3 ft. in
length forms the bottom bridle loop; and a piece which is 2 ft. in
length is used for the top loop. Tie the bottom loop at positions
which are about 7 in. from the bottom of the crossbars and the

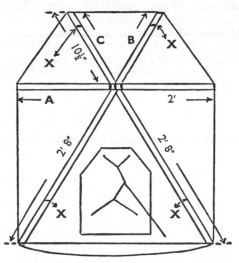

FIG. 5. High flyer (No. 2)

top loop about 3 in. from the top of the crossbars. These loops
are connected by means of string which is 2 ft. 10 in. in length.
Tie the kite line to this by means of a bowline knot and a reef
knot. Take another piece of string, 2 ft. 9 in. in length and tie it
in the form of a loop to the bottom of the crossbars. A tail, about
5 ft. in length, is tied to the centre of this loop.

This kite may be readily dismantled if the two crossbars are
joined together by means of a nail which acts as a pivot. The
horizontal bar is held in place by means of string, bound round,
which on being untied, permits the bar to be withdrawn and the
crossbars to be folded together. The cover may then be rolled
up round the crossbars, and tied with a piece of tape.

THE HEXAGONAL KITE

This is a simple flat wing kite, which can be readily adapted to different sizes. It has a lively performance, and does well in a gentle breeze. It is one of the class which is not bow shaped. This bow shape forms what is called the dihedral angle, and as we have seen in the comments upon the Tonking kite, dihedral improves stability. On the face of it, therefore, it would seem that the Hexagonal kite will not be so steady in flight as those which are bow shaped. But the reader will observe the way in which the bridle is tied. The purpose of this is to provide some stability in flight. This stability is further improved by the use of a flexible tail.

The framework is formed by three pieces, A, B, and C. These are 2 ft. 6 in. in length, and are cut from ⅜ in. square stripwood. Slightly notch the ends of the pieces, at D (Fig. 6). These provide a seating for the string bracing. Make halving joints at the positions indicated (E, Fig. 6). These joints will have to be made with care, so that the saw cuts do not go too deep, and the pieces fit snugly. Use a fretsaw with a fine blade for this. Join the pieces with glue, after smoothing them thoroughly with fine sandpaper. It is recommended that cross-shaped strengtheners, cut from ⅛ in. plywood, be fixed over these joints with glue and thread, as shown at F (Fig. 6). The completed framework should be smooth, firm and straight.

Next, add the bracing. Use thin strong string, which must be quite taut. To achieve this, make a temporary support as shown at G (Fig. 6), and lash it to the framework. Now tie the string to the top left-hand strut. Take it to the top right-hand strut, bind round and tie. From there, in the same manner, take the string to the other ends of the framework, and complete the bracing by tying at the point where you started. Remove the support. The bracing needs to be carefully and neatly done, to maintain the framework in the right shape, and to provide a firm support for the covering material.

The cover is made of unbleached greaseproof paper. It is chosen for its strength and lightness—very important factors. The paper is generally obtained in sheets measuring 20 in. × 30 in. so two of them will have to be joined together to give the required

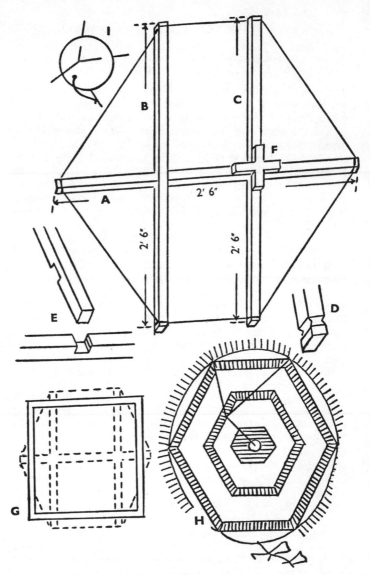

FIG. 6. Hexagonal

width. Lay the framework on the paper and mark the shape of the kite with a pencil. Add a margin of $1\frac{1}{2}$ in. all round for over-lapping, and cut out. At this point the cover may be decorated. A simple design is suggested at H (Fig. 6). Strips of coloured paper of the same kind and glued on, may be used. Other designs are given in 'Accessories'.

Attach the cover to the framework. Apply glue to the outer half of the margin, fold this over the strings and fasten down. Please note that the cover, in order to be perfectly flat, is fixed to the framework on the reverse side of the cross-shaped strengthening pieces. Cut 3 in. wide strips of paper and glue these to the inside of the cover over the framework. They will help to strengthen the cover against the pressure of the wind.

Pierce the cover at the centre, so that the bottom bridle string can be threaded through. Cut a hexagonal-shaped piece of thin cardboard, pierce it through the centre, and glue it to the centre of the cover. Take a 3 ft. length of strong string and tie it securely to the centre of the framework, passing it through the cardboard shape.

A loop of string completes the bridle. For this use a piece 4 ft. 6 in. in length, and tie it to the top ends of the vertical struts. Tie the bottom string to the centre of the loop. The kite line is attached to the bottom string by means of a bowline knot and a reef knot.

An alternative method is shown at I (Fig. 6). Cut a 3 in. diameter circle from $\frac{3}{16}$ in. plywood. Drill holes through it at the positions shown. Thread the top loop through the top holes, and tie the kite line to it. Thread the other bridle string through the bottom hole and knot it, using a bowline knot. This will permit of adjustments being made, by lengthening or shortening the bottom bridle string.

The tail which is 6 ft. in length is attached to a loop of string tied to the bottom ends of the vertical struts. A paper tassel can be fitted to the end of the tail.

Further decoration may be in the form of fringes cut from paper 12 in. wide and folded and pasted together to form a double thickness. These are fastened over strings tied in the positions shown. The colour of the fringes should match the general decoration scheme.

By way of further comment it may be said that this kite should take-off successfully from the hand, without outside help. Success in flying depends upon the right amount of tail. For example, if the kite moves unsteadily, then the weight of the tail must be increased by adding extra paper pieces. On the other hand, if it does not lift, and tends to drag down to the ground, then the tail must be lightened. The position of the kite line is important. Generally it is tied a little above the centre of gravity. This centre may be ascertained by using the method described in Chapter 8, and also mentioned in the instructions for the Pegtop kite. A little practice will soon show what adjustments to make.

CHAPTER THREE

Star: Three-T: Forktop

THE STAR KITE

THIS pretty kite possesses two interesting features. One is that there is a centre piece of metal foil, which reflects the light; this is an effective decorative device. The other feature is that the kite is equipped with balancing cups, to assist its flight. The cups help to produce up-currents of air which give lift to the kite. Consequently, it should do well in a light breeze. Being designed for gentle weather, the kite is lightly constructed. The framework is comparatively slender. The kite must be handled with care.

As will be seen in Fig. 7, it is formed with a double frame—a diamond and a cross shape. The frame, A, is made first. Use $\frac{1}{4}$ in. × $\frac{3}{16}$ in. stripwood. Cut four pieces, each 1 ft. 5 in. in length. Assemble them in the shape of a square, by means of mitre joints. Small corner pieces, cut from $\frac{1}{8}$ in. plywood to the shape of a triangle are fixed to the underside of the joints with glue and fine fretwork nails. An alternative method of joining the frame is also shown (B, Fig. 7). In this method, two of the strips measure 1 ft. 4$\frac{1}{2}$ in. Secure these joints also with glue and fine fretwork nails. Drill holes to receive the nails part-way through the wood, so that it will not split. Make the joints as firm as possible, in view of the fact that this is the main frame.

The cross-shaped frame C (Fig. 7) requires three pieces $\frac{1}{4}$ in. × $\frac{3}{16}$ in. stripwood, D and E. Cut D, 2 ft. in length, groove the ends, and drill a small hole through, $\frac{1}{2}$ in. from the bottom end. Fix this to the underside of the frame A, in the position shown, with glue and two $\frac{3}{4}$ in. fretwork nails, the ends of which are turned over and hammered flat. This strut divides the frame, A, into two equal parts.

You will need next a centre-piece, F, which is cut from $\frac{1}{8}$ in. plywood and is 2 in. square. Glue and nail it to the underside centre of the strut D. Use $\frac{5}{8}$ in. fretwork nails, bent over and flattened at the ends. To this centre-piece and to the frame, A, glue and nail the two short cross-struts, E. Each measures 11$\frac{7}{8}$ in.

29

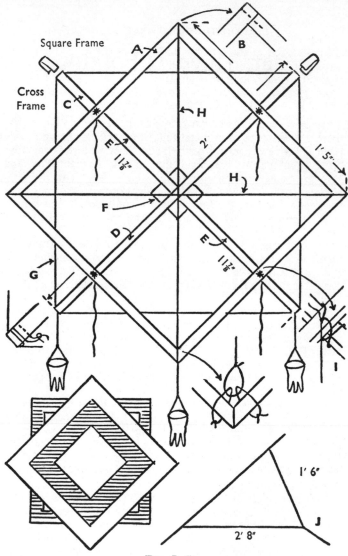

FIG. 7. Star

and is notched at the outer end. The idea of using two short pieces, is that they fit flush with the frame, A, which would not be possible with a long through strut.

The bracing string, G, is added next. Thin strong string, knotted at one end is used. Thread it through the hole at the end of D (Fig. 7). Pass it in turn over the ends of the cross-struts. Bring it back to where you started. Bind it round the strut end once or twice and tie at the first knot. Strips of insulating tape neatly applied, will hold the string in place in their grooves. Apply tape also where the string crosses the main frame A. Keep the string taut, but do not pull the framework out of shape. Note that the bracing lies on the underside of the frame A.

The inner strings, G and H, come on the top side of the framework. They go from corner to corner. As these are difficult tying places, a special method is used. Loops of string are made at the corners. To them the bracing string is attached by means of another loop (see Fig. 7). It will be realized that on the actual kite, these loops are drawn up and fastened securely.

The bridle is of string which is stouter than that used for the bracing. Four pieces are needed. Two are 1 ft. 9 in., and two, 2 ft. 11 in. in length. The tying points on the framework are indicated by asterisks. These points have been chosen to improve the stability of the kite and also because they represent the strongest parts of the framework and so are the obvious points to take up the strain in flying the kite. The shorter strings are fastened at the top points. The method of securing the strings to the framework is shown in detail at I (Fig. 7). J (Fig. 7) shows actual length of bridle strings when they are tied.

Next cover the framework with unbleached greaseproof paper. First attend to the small triangles formed by the ends of the cross-struts and the bracing. Cut four pieces, measuring 8 in. at the base and $4\frac{1}{4}$ in. high, narrowing to a point. Glue these to the top sides of A; also to the cross-struts, and wrap over the strings. The main cover is 1 ft. $5\frac{1}{2}$ in. square and is glued to the sides of A. Turn the kite over and glue strips of paper to the underside, over the strings G and H.

The result should be a secure, well-stretched cover, and with this type of kite, this should not be difficult to achieve, as the framework is all on one level, and is not bowed.

There are several ways in which the kite can be decorated,

according to preference. A simple and pleasing way is shown in Fig. 7. Broad bands of bright colours are used. A square of metal foil previously mentioned, silver or gold, is glued at the centre. This will shine and flash in the light. It will be easier to do the decorating before the cover is fixed in place.

A feature of this kite is its use of three balancing cups, 3 in. in diameter, attached to the lower ends of the framework. They are described in detail in the section on 'Accessories' and are decorative as well as serving a useful purpose.

The strings which hold these are about 6 in. in length after they have been tied in place, and before the cover is added. Alternatively, paper tassels may be used. Details for making both of these are given in Chapter 7 in 'Accessories'.

Tie the kite string to the bridle, where it is knotted together. This method does not permit of the line being adjusted on the bridle as is the case with many of the kites described. Such adjustments are made to alter the angle of the kite to the wind. Therefore to keep the kite at a proper flying angle it may be found helpful to fit a tail. The line for this could run through the centre balancing cup, and it would be about 5 ft. in length. This tail could be regarded as additional equipment which could be fixed or removed as required. Therefore it would be tied in such a way that the knot be easily undone.

Again, practice in flying the kite would soon indicate what adjustments should be made in this direction, that is to say whether a tail were needed or not, or whether the tail should be made heavier or lighter by adding or removing some of the paper pieces.

The Three-T Kite

As the name implies, this kite is an arrangement of three triangles, which give it a rather unusual look. It is a flat-type form which depends for stability upon a two-piece bridle and a flexible tail.

The backbone, A (Fig. 8), is 2 ft. 10 in. in length, and is cut from ⅜ in. square stripwood, which must be straight and smooth. Drill holes ½ in. from each end, through which the bracing string is threaded. The ends are also notched, as shown. Two pieces of ⅜ in. square stripwood are used for the crossbars, B and C. The top crossbar, B (Fig. 8) is 2 ft. in length, and the lower one, C

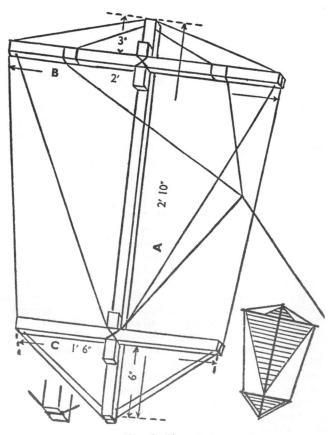

3"

B

2'

2' 10"

A

C   1' 6"

6"

FIG. 8. Three-T

(Fig. 8) is 1 ft. 6 in. Drill and notch the ends as in the case of the backbone.

Fix the crossbars to the backbone, B, 3 in. from the top, and C, 6 in. from the bottom. Use glue and strong thread to make firm joints. Glue small blocks to the backbone on each side of the crossbars to help to keep them straight.

The bracing is added next. Begin at the top of the framework and tie a length of thin strong string to the top crossbar, 6 in. from one end. Thread this through the hole in the backbone, and tie to the other side of the crossbar, 6 in. from the end. Next, pass a length through one of the holes in the top crossbar, and tie one end. Take the string to a position on the backbone, which is 6½ in. from the bottom end. Bind it round the bottom crossbar once or twice, and take it to the other end of the top crossbar, where it is threaded through the hole and tied. Tie a length of string to one end of the bottom crossbar, after passing it through the hole, and tie. Then thread it through the holes in the ends of the backbone and crossbar and tie. A secondary bracing string is run round the edges of the framework, making use of the grooves provided. The bracing should be taut, in order to provide a firm foundation for the covers, and to keep the framework in its proper shape.

The cover is added in three separate pieces. Use unbleached greaseproof paper, or lightweight cotton material such as cambric. Cut pieces for the top triangle, which forms the nose; for the large triangle, which forms the wing, and for the smaller tail-piece. Lay the framework upon the material and mark the shapes. Allow a margin of 1 in. all round and cut out.

At this point the covers may be decorated if desired. Suggestions for designs are given in Chapter 7. Use fabric painting oil colours for cloth, and lacquer for paper. Pin the covers to a board while the decorating is being done, and allow sufficient time for the paints to dry before doing anything else.

Next, glue the nose cover to the top crossbar and round the inner top bracing strings. Add the wing and tail covers in the same way. If cloth covers are used, then the margins are sewn down over the bracing strings. Like paper covers, they would, of course, be glued to the crossbars.

Two pieces of strong string are used to make the bridle. One piece, which is 2 ft. 6 in. in length is tied to the top crossbar, 5 in. from each end. The second piece, which is 3 ft. 3 in. is tied to the bottom backbone joint and then to the centre of the other piece. Attach the kite line to the bottom bridle string by means of a bowline knot, and a reef knot.

The tail which is fixed to the bottom of the backbone is 6 ft. in length. If desired paper fringes may be run round the outer bracing strings. Use strips of paper, 4 in. in width, fold them down the centre, glue them round the strings, and cut in narrow fingers to form the fringe.

THE FORKTOP KITE

This kite is given its name because its backbone is divided into two curved prongs at the top. It has the double advantage of being bow shaped, and possessing a large sail area. The operator will find that it will move in a lively manner. Correct balance and shape are essential for successful flying. These are achieved by paying careful attention to all the constructional details. It is one of the largest kites described in the book, consequently the bridle and kite line must be correspondingly strong.

The backbone, A, is 3 ft. 6 in. in length. Use $\frac{3}{8}$ in. square strip-wood, which should be straight and smooth, and free from knots or any other defect. Notch the ends as shown (Fig. 9) and with a fine fretsaw blade saw down from the top end to a depth of 6 in. This makes two prongs, which are bent to a fork shape. First, soak the prongs in water for about an hour. Then bind round the backbone just below the prongs with strong thread. This will prevent the saw cut from developing into a split. Now, gently but firmly prise the prongs apart, and insert a wedge at the top of the opening. Use a piece of stripwood $\frac{3}{8}$ in. square × 1 in. Glue and nail it in place. and drill small holes to start the fretwork nails, which are $\frac{1}{2}$ in. long.

The crossbar, B, is 3 ft. in length. Use split cane about $\frac{1}{4}$ in. thick, or as an alternative, $\frac{1}{4}$ in. square stripwood. The ends are grooved and two small holes are drilled through, $\frac{1}{2}$ in. from each end. Following this, the crossbar is curved to a bow shape. If cane is used, apply dry heat, for example, a gas jet, whilst bending it. This will stop it splitting. Soaking for a while in water is recommended if stripwood is used. See the section on 'Methods' in Chapter 7.

Details of the shaping are as follows. Take a length of good

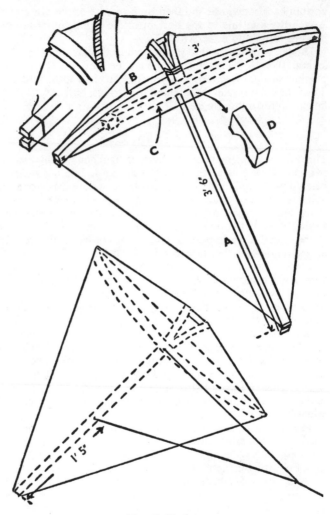

FIG. 9. Forktop

quality string. Thread it through one of the holes and tie it, leaving a 5 in. tail to the knot. Pass the string over the end of the crossbar and over to the other end, where it is threaded through the second hole. Applying firm pressure, bend the crossbar to a curve. To do this rest one end of it on the floor. Press firmly downwards, at the same time drawing the string taut. Bind the end of this once or twice round the crossbar and tie. The depth of the curve at the centre should be about 3 in. This bowstring has to withstand considerable strain so make sure that it is tough.

The next stage is to attach the crossbar to the backbone, 7 in. from the top. Two small anchor blocks, each measuring $\frac{1}{4}$ in. $\times$ $\frac{3}{8}$ in. $\times$ 1 in. are glued to the backbone on either side of the crossbar. The latter is then glued and also lashed in place with thin string. Smear the binding with glue to stiffen it. Treat all subsequent bindings in the same way. It is highly important that the joint be properly made, for upon it depends the firmness of the framework.

The framework is now ready to be braced. Use thin string which is capable of withstanding considerable strain. Tie a length to the bowstring, making use of the 5 in. tail which has been left. Pass it over the top end of the backbone, bind it round the other end of the crossbar and tie securely. Check that the bracing is really taut. Next, tie a length of string to one end of the crossbar, pass it over the bottom end of the backbone, and pass round and tie to the end of the crossbar. The finished bracing should sound a musical note when plucked with the fingers.

If stripwood is used for the crossbar, a reinforcing strip is used, C. This is 1 ft. 5 in. in length and is cut from $\frac{1}{4}$ in. square stripwood. This is placed between two small anchor blocks of the same wood, 1 in. in length, which are glued to the crossbar. The centre of the strip comes over the centre of the backbone. Bind the ends of the strip, and also the blocks, to the crossbar with thin string. A small stripwood bridge, D, is placed between the backbone and the reinforcing strip, and is held in place with glue and a small fretwork nail.

The bridle is attached to the backbone in the form of a loop. Tying points are shown in Fig. 9. Use stout string, 7 ft. in length. A small anchor block is glued underneath the bottom tying point to prevent the bridle from slipping down.

The framework is covered with pure unbleached greaseproof

paper, or better still, lightweight cotton material. It may be necessary to join two pieces of the material together to make the cover. Lay the frame upon the material and with a soft grade pencil, mark out the shape allowing a margin of 2 in. all round for overlapping, and cut out. Cut narrow V-shaped slits in the margin.

The cover may be decorated at this stage. A bright bold design looks most effective. Small details are useless. A pleasing design is illustrated in Chapter 7 under the heading 'Accessories'. It is advisable to produce the design on a separate piece of paper if a paper cover is used, and then glue it in place. One of the proprietary brands of lacquer goes well on paper and is easy to apply. If a cloth cover is used, then either a paper pattern may be glued on, as above, or the design may be painted on direct, using fabric painting oil colours.

Apply glue to the backbone and the crossbar and lay the cover in place. If it is a paper cover, apply glue to the outer half of the margin, fold over the bracing strings and fasten down. A cloth cover is sewn down. Note that the cover is divided at the top by the prongs. Glue extra strips of material around these for strengthening.

The kite line is attached to the bridle by means of a bowline knot and a reef knot. The line is generally located a little way above the centre of gravity. To find this, place the kite by its backbone upon the end of a stick. The point at which the kite balances is the centre of gravity.

A tail is fitted which is about 7 ft. in length. Two tassels may be suspended on strings from the ends of the crossbars. The ends of the framework should be protected by strips of insulating tape.

It may be said, by way of general comment, that this kite is of the traditional style which is a great favourite because of its satisfactory performance. To achieve the latter, however, it may be found necessary to make certain adjustments, such as altering the position of the line on the bridle, or increasing or decreasing the weight of the tail by adding or removing paper pieces.

CHAPTER FOUR

Festoon: Happy Man: Small Fish

THE FESTOON KITE

THIS kite looks very attractive in flight, and is one which is well worth making. It is a combined kite, that is, two kites arranged on one backbone. It has a comparatively slender framework and needs to be handled with care.

The backbone, A, is 3 ft. 6 in. in length, and is cut from ⅜ in. square stripwood. Make halving joints, 6 in. from the top and 1 ft. 6 in. from the bottom (see Fig. 10). Make shallow grooves at points which are ½ in. and 3 in. from each end and also one at the centre.

Two crossbars, B and C, are each 2 ft. in length, and are cut from ⅜ in. × ¼ in. stripwood. Complete the halving joints at the centre of these, and also make shallow grooves at points which are 3 in. and again ½ in. from each end. Rub the frame pieces to a smooth finish with fine sandpaper, and check that the joints are a tight fit.

Assemble the framework with glue. Strengthen the joints by gluing cross-shaped plates to the underside. These are formed from ⅛ in. plywood. They are 6 in. in length and 6 in. in width (see Fig. 10). Bind round the plates and the joints with fine string, and smear the binding with thin glue to hold it in place.

Brace the framework with thin strong string. Tie a length to the backbone at the point D, and take it to the groove E, which is 3 in. from the right-hand end of the top crossbar, pass it round once or twice and tie. Bring the string to the centre backbone groove, bind round and tie. From there take it to the groove which is 3 in. from the left-hand end of the top crossbar, and lastly to the point where you started, where the string is securely tied. Repeat the procedure for the lower half of the framework. The outer bracing strings are now added, being secured at the grooves which are at the ends of the frame pieces. There should be an even tension on all these strings,

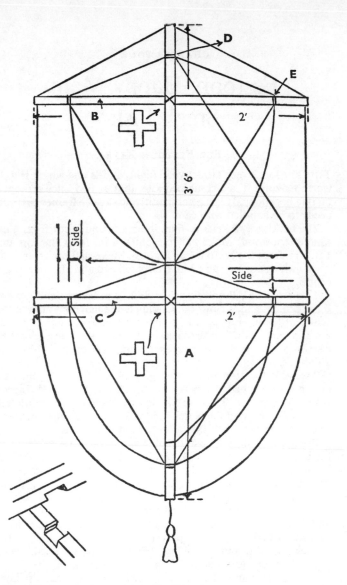

FIG. 10. Festoon

and the backbone and crossbars should be at a correct angle.

The next step is to prepare the covers. Cambric or unbleached greaseproof paper may be used. Lay the framework on the material and draw the shapes with a soft-grade pencil, allowing a margin of 2 in. all round for overlapping. It is a help to pin the material to a board whilst this is being done. The covers may be decorated at this stage. Suggested designs are given in Chapter 7, under 'Accessories'. Use fabric painting oil colours for cloth, and lacquer for paper covers. Allow sufficient time for the paint to dry and then cut out.

Attach the covers to the backbone and crossbars with glue. Fold the margins over the inner bracing strings and fasten down. Use glue for paper, and sew down in the case of cloth covers. The covers should be as firm and smooth as possible. Turn the framework over. Prepare 2 in. strips of the material and glue them to the covers and around the framework within the area required.

Decorate the kite with festoons. To do this, tie lengths of strong thread in the form of three loops, at the points shown. Take strips of paper 2 in. in width and 6 in. in length, fold them down the centre, and cut slits at intervals in the centre fold. Now cut the strips in fingers to make the fringes. Open the strips, apply glue down the centre and wrap around the loops. Cover the outer bracing string for the top kite with fringes. A paper tassel on a 1 ft. length of thread is suspended from the bottom of the backbone. A pennant may also be flown from the top of the backbone. See 'Accessories', Chapter 7, for making these.

The bridle is tied to the backbone in the form of a loop at the positions shown (Fig. 10). Use strong string, 6 ft. in length. The kite line is attached to the bridle with a bowline knot and a reef knot. Apply strips of insulating tape to the ends of the framework, to prevent their splitting, should the kite hit the ground suddenly.

Like other kites, this one will need adjustments of the kite line in order to achieve satisfactory flight. Apart from regulating the position of this line, other adjustments may take the form of lengthening the tassel string, or sometimes using a thicker string. The increase of weight thus obtained will tend to pull the bottom of the kite down. This action will bring the kite nearer to the vertical, if the flying angle is too shallow, that is, if the kite is· inclined too much towards the horizontal. When a kite assumes a shallow angle it will not climb. If on the other hand, the tail is too heavy, the kite will assume a near vertical position, and by reason of this will tend to be blown backwards by the wind meanwhile gradually losing height. It is essential that the correct flying angle be established, and this is achieved mainly by observation and adjustment.

THE HAPPY MAN KITE

Kites are made in a variety of shapes and sizes. Some are conventional, such as the box and the pegtop; others are more original, and to this class the Happy Man Kite belongs. It is a humorous novelty and will cause some amusement when it is flying in the air. A novel feature is the imitation ladder, which takes the place of a conventional tail. The little man has indeed climbed to the top, hence his smile of achievement. Much of the appeal of the kite depends upon the making of the figure. To simplify this, a pattern for enlarging is given (Fig. 11).

Though the kite is unusual in form, the principle of sound design and structure have been kept in mind. First, there is a broad cover area for buoyancy. Secondly, the kite is bowed in the interests of dihedral, which improves stability. Thirdly, the ladder-tail is more than a novelty; it improves stability, by helping to keep the kite on the right course.

Begin by making the framework. The backbone, A, is cut from $\frac{3}{8}$ in. square stripwood, which must be straight and free from blemish. It is 3 ft. in length, and is grooved slightly at the ends. The positions for the crossbars are marked on it. Measuring from the top in each case, these positions are: one, $5\frac{1}{2}$ in.; two, 1 ft. $3\frac{1}{2}$ in.; three, 1 ft. $8\frac{1}{2}$ in., and four, 2 ft. $6\frac{1}{2}$ in.

Now prepare the crossbars B, C, D, and E. All are formed from split cane, about $\frac{1}{4}$ in. thick. They are grooved at the ends. B and D are 2 ft. 1 in. in length; and C and E are 1 ft. 1 in. Drill small holes through, $\frac{1}{2}$ in. from the ends. Next, form them into a bow shape. Bend them into shape by firm but gentle pressure of the hands. The application of dry heat in the form of a gas jet or electric fire may also be helpful in conditioning the cane for bending. The curved shapes are retained by means of bowstrings which are threaded through the holes provided, and tied securely. Draw the bowstrings taut in order to achieve a proper tension on the canes. Leave a 5 in. tail to one of the bowstrings at F. The

FIG. 11. Happy man

depth of the curve at the centre of B and D is $2\frac{1}{2}$ in.; and there is a proportionate depth for C and E. This depth is achieved by bending C and E until their curves match B and D.

Secure the crossbars to the backbone at the places which are marked. Glue small blocks to the backbone on either side of the bars, to help to keep them in the right position. Glue and bind the crossbars to the backbone. Smear the bindings with thin glue to reinforce them. Note that the bowstrings lie clear of the backbone on the underside of the framework (Fig. 12).

Use thin string for the outline bracing. Tie a length to the bowstring tail marked F. Take it over the crossbar B; over the top of the backbone, and to the other end of C. Bind round and tie. Proceed by taking the string to the other ends of the framework, and bind round once or twice in each case. Finish by tying to the bowstring tail where you started. Check that the bracing string is taut and that the crossbars are level.

Use lightweight cotton material, such as cambric, for the cover. A square yard will be sufficient. Fasten it to a board with drawing pins. Now take a sheet of paper and mark on it a pattern of 5 in. squares. On this, enlarge the figure which is illustrated in Fig. 11. Allow for a margin of 2 in. all round. The sides of the feet, the arms, ears and top of the head are drawn separately and are attached by the overlaps indicated by the dotted lines.

Pin the paper pattern on the cloth and by means of carbon paper transfer the drawing to the cloth. When this has been done, paint the figure in suitable colours, using fabric painting oil colours. Allow sufficient time for the paint to dry, and then cut out, not forgetting to include the margin.

Fasten the cover to the crossbars with glue. Fold the margin over the bracing strings and sew down. See that the cover is evenly stretched and neatly secured. Next, take the separate parts, such as the arms and ears, and glue them on to thin cardboard for stiffening. Attach them with glue at the positions shown by the dotted lines.

The bridle string is tied in the form of a loop at the points marked X in Fig. 12. Strong string, 6 ft. in length will be needed. Pierce the cover in the appropriate places, and thread the string through. Glue small cloth washers to the cover where it is pierced, to prevent the material fraying. The kite line is attached to the bridle by means of a bowline knot and a reef knot.

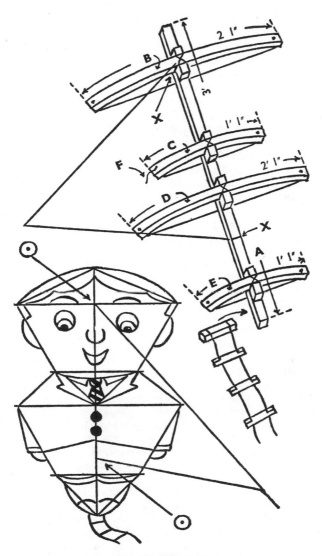

FIG. 12. Happy man

Two ladder strings, 6 ft. in length, are tied to the small bar which is glued and nailed to the bottom of the backbone. This ¼ in. square stripwood bar is 5 in. in length, and the strings are placed 4 in. apart. The rungs are made from strips of cardboard, and are 5 in. in length. At the ends of these make slits, and insert the strings. Space the rungs about 6 in. apart. A little practice will soon indicate the correct number to carry for a flight, for which reason they are made to be removed or replaced easily.

The kite is fairly large in size, and develops quite a strong pull in a wind. The bridle and the line must be adequate to meet the strain which is imposed. The young reader is advised not to allow such a kite to attain too great a height or fly it in too strong a wind.

THE SMALL FISH KITE

Here is a kite of unusual design, which looks very attractive in flight. The time and care needed in the construction will be amply repaid by its performance. Being a multi-frame type, it is important to maintain the correct proportions of every part.

The first stage is to make the framework. The backbone A, in ¼ in. square stripwood, is 1 ft. 6 in. in length. The crossbars, B, C, and D are formed from thin split cane. B is 1 ft. 3 in. in length, and C and D are 1 ft. Groove them at the ends. The crossbars must now be formed in a bow shape. This is achieved by applying dry heat to the bars whilst the shaping is being done. The curve is retained by means of bowstrings, tied to each end of the bars. The depth of the curve for the largest crossbar is 1½ in. at the centre, and the curves on the other two must correspond to this. Check that this is so by laying the smaller bars in turn on the larger one. The curves on all the canes should match.

Fix the crossbars to the backbone. The larger one is lashed to the centre of the backbone. The two smaller ones are attached at points 3 in. from the top and the bottom of the backbone. Glue ½ in. blocks of stripwood to the latter on either side of the crossbars, to help to hold them in place. Smear the binding string with glue to stiffen it, and treat all further bindings in the same way.

Centre cane, such as is used in basketry and cane furniture, is used for the shaped framework, because it is easy to form in sharp curves. Use cane which is 3 mm. in diameter, and before

shaping it, soak it in water for an hour. The outer curve, E, requires a piece which is 4 ft. in length. Lash it at its centre to a
point which is near to the top of the backbone. Glue a small stripwood block to the backbone just below and touching the joint,
which will act as a buffer for the cane. Cover the joint with a
glued strip of cloth, and treat all the ends of the framework in
the same way, as shown in Fig. 13.

Now with a pencil mark a position which is $2\frac{1}{4}$ in. from each
end of the centre crossbar. Glue small blocks to the bar, on the
inside of the pencil marks. Bend the cane round, so that it rests
against the blocks, and lash it securely in place. Next, bring the
cane down to a position which is 3 in. from each end of the bottom
crossbar, and tie securely. Complete the shaping by bringing the
cane to the bottom of the backbone, bind round and tie. In order
to make a neat bottom joint, score the cane with a sharp knife,
$\frac{1}{2}$ in. from its ends, and with the knife, shave the ends of the cane
flat to a length of $\frac{1}{2}$ in. The ends will now quite easily bend to a
sharp angle, to fit flush with the backbone (see Fig. 13). Now
secure the cane to the top crossbar with strong thread.

Next mark on the backbone a position which is $3\frac{1}{2}$ in. from the
top. Place the ruler on this position so that it lies across the
framework, parallel to the crossbars, and mark corresponding
positions on the outer curved cane. These marks indicate where
the inner curves, F and G, are fixed. The two canes required for
this measure 2 ft. in length. Flatten the ends of these to a length
of $\frac{1}{2}$ in. with a sharp knife and flatten slightly the curved cane, E,
on the inside by the pencil marks. Begin the shaping with the
cane, F. Glue and bind one end to the outer curve, E. Bring the
cane in a curve across the backbone at the point which is marked
off in pencil. Flatten the cane slightly where it rests on the backbone. Glue it down and further hold it in place with one or two
turns of thread. Glue small blocks to the backbone on each side
of the cane. Now bring the other cane, G, to the same position
and lash the two canes securely to the backbone with strong
thread.

Take the cane, F, in a continuing curve to a point on the centre
crossbar, which is 1 in. from the backbone. Place a small block
under the cane at this point. The end of the cane is brought to
the right-hand end of the bottom crossbar, to which it is securely
bound. Repeat the procedure for the other cane. Note that where

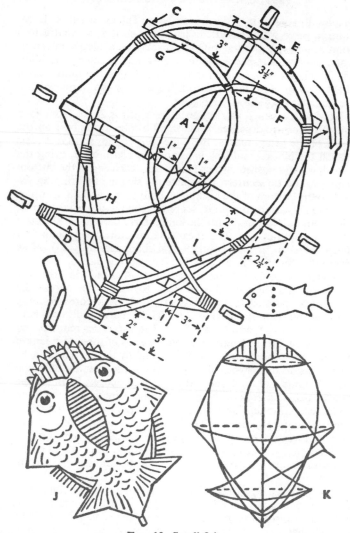

FIG. 13. Small fish

this cane crosses the centre crossbar, a small block is inserted to fill the gap.

Two other curved parts, H and I, are needed to complete the framework. They are each 10 in. in length and are flattened at both their ends. Bind them to the outer curve, 2 in. below the centre crossbar, and also to the backbone, 2 in. from the bottom. Check all the joints to make sure they are firm, and make sure that all the curves correspond on each side of the backbone.

The framework is now ready to be braced. Tie a length of fine string to the end of the top crossbar. Take it over the end of the centre bar, and tie at the joint below it. Repeat the procedure for the other side. Next tie a length of string to the end of the bottom crossbar and tie to the backbone where the inner canes are joined. From there, take it to the other end of the crossbar, and tie. Make the bracing strings taut.

At this stage, prepare the cover. Lay the framework on a sheet of unbleached greaseproof paper, and draw the shape as at J. Add a margin of 1 in. all round for overlapping and cut out. It is a matter of choice whether or not the small curved centre-piece is cut out. Slit the margin at intervals to make the work of wrapping it round the framework easier.

The cover may now be decorated. Eyes, scales, and fin marks may be painted in blue on a background of aluminium paint. Allow the paint to dry thoroughly and then glue the cover to the framework and bracing strings.

The bridle is formed of thin strong string, which is 3 ft. 6 in. in length. Secure it to the backbone in the form of a loop at the positions shown at K (Fig. 13). The kite line is attached to the bridle by means of a bowline knot and a reef knot. See 'Knots' in Chapter 7.

This kite requires a tail which is 4 ft. 6 in. in length. Small fish, 5 in. long by 2½ in. wide, cut from thin cardboard and having four small holes punched down the centre, are used for the tail pieces. They are spaced 5 in. or 6 in. apart, and are threaded on to the string by means of the holes. Tie a bow at the bottom of the string. The tail fish match the general colour scheme, for example, one blue, the next aluminium and so on.

J and K (Fig. 13) show additional decoration to the kite. This is in the form of strips of paper attached to strings, which are fastened to the top curve of E, and to the top curves of F and G.

A large fish kite may be made by doubling all the measurements given. In this case ⅜ in. square stripwood and 5 mm. centre cane would be used, and stronger string would be needed for the bridle and kite line. One could also use lightweight cloth instead of paper for the cover.

CHAPTER FIVE

Butterfly: Double Butterfly: Glider

BUTTERFLY KITE

THIS, one of the prettiest of all kites, is quite simple to make. There is a minimum of framework and the covering is quite straightforward. It can be strikingly decorated. Altogether it is a kite you will want to make.

The framework comprises a backbone, A, and two curved pieces, B and C. For A use $\frac{3}{4}$ in. × $\frac{1}{4}$ in. stripwood, 2 ft. 8 in. in length. It is notched at the ends. B and C are formed from 8 mm. centre cane (round cane) as used in basketry and cane furniture. This should be soaked in water beforehand to condition it. Two pieces, each 4 ft. 8 in. in length are required and they are grooved at the ends to provide a hold for the bracing strings.

First shape the two curves. Smear one end of B with thin glue and when it is tacky, tie a length of thin, strong string in the groove, bind round once or twice and tie again. Bend the cane in the form of a part circle as shown in Fig. 14. Bind round and tie the string at the other end, first smearing it with glue to prevent the binding from slipping out of place, D. As you proceed, apply glue at all points where the strings are tied. The length of this string after it has been tied will be about 2 ft. 1 in., D. Tie a second string from the bottom end of curved-shape B to a point which is 6 in. from the top end, Z. The length of this string, E, after it has been tied in place, will be about 2 ft. 3 in.

Shape C in the same manner. Lay one cane upon the other to check that the curves are the same. The shaping of these must be done with care, and without undue force.

Next assemble the framework. Bind round and tie B at points which are 6 in. from the top and 6 in. from the bottom of the backbone. Use fine string or strong carpet thread. A small inner curve is thus formed. The depth of this curve at the centre, measuring from the backbone, is about 3 in. Fix C in position in the same way. Bind round and tie the strings F and G at the

51

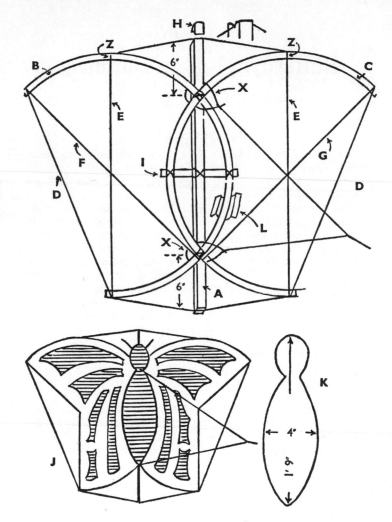

FIG. 14. Butterfly

positions indicated (Fig. 14). Run strings over the ends of the backbone. Glue cloth strips over the ends to hold the bracing in place, H.

The discerning reader will notice on looking at the framework that there is a danger of the kite folding up in flight because of wind pressure on the wings. To prevent this, the following device is fitted. Take a piece of stripwood about 8 in. long and glue and bind it to the underside centre of the backbone. Now glue and insert small blocks to fill up the gaps between this strip and the curved canes. Then bind the canes and the strips together with stout thread. See I (Fig. 14) for details. This device will prevent undue movement of the wings in flight.

The next stage is to cover the framework, where required. A glance at J (Fig. 14) will make this clear. Use paper which is light but strong (unbleached greaseproof is recommended). This is generally obtained in sheets measuring 20 in. × 30 in. First join two of them together with thin glue down the centre. Lay the framework on the paper and make an outline with a soft grade pencil. Add a margin of 2 in. all round for overlapping and cut out. Make slits in the margin. This will help when pasting the cover down. Cut out the head and body in card, the thickness of a postcard (see J and K, Fig. 14). Decorate the covering in bright colours, using oil colours for permanence. These look well on foundations of aluminium paint. After these have dried, secure the covering to the framework, the margins overlapping the canes and inner strings. Try to obtain a taut smooth surface. Add the head and body, using thin glue. Turn the kite over and glue strips 1 in. wide and $2\frac{1}{2}$ in. long, at intervals over the small centre curves, and to the cover, as indicated by L (Fig. 14). Two pipe cleaners are glued to the backbone, to stick out above the head, forming the antennae.

The bridle is attached in the form of a loop at the points marked (Fig. 14). Use strong string, 5 ft. in length. It is important to note that this string is looped round the backbone and tied over the centre junctions, Fig. 14 will make this clear. The loose loops are shown for the sake of detail. They must, of course, be tightened up on the kite itself. These tying positions are the strongest points at which to take up the strain imposed when flying the kite. Unless this rule is observed, the result might be a broken backbone. As will be seen, to attach the bridle, it is necessary to pierce the covering. Do this carefully and glue small thin cardboard washers over the holes to strengthen material.

The kite string is attached to the bridle by means of a reef knot and a bowline knot. These permit of adjustments being made on the bridle to keep the kite at the best angle for successful flight. This is explained in more detail in Chapter 8.

A short tail about 5 ft. in length is required. Details for making these are given in 'Accessories'.

DOUBLE BUTTERFLY KITE

This pretty kite is a development of the one previously described. The framework is necessarily more elaborate, and so the instructions must be followed carefully. The kite is one of which you may be proud, both for its appearance and performance.

The backbone, A, is 2 ft. 9 in. in length and is cut from $\frac{3}{8}$ in. square stripwood, which must be straight and free from blemish. The main wing curves, B and C, are formed from 8 mm. centre cane. They are each 4 ft. 7 in. in length. It is an advantage, for the sake of lightness and fixing to split about one-third of the cane off with a sharp-pointed knife. All the cane used, prior to its being assembled, should be soaked in water for an hour or so (see Fig. 15.)

Glue and tie the cane, B, to a point which is 3 in. from the top of the backbone and 1 ft. 4 in. from the top end of the cane. Bring the cane round in a curve, glue, bind round and tie again at a point which is 3 in. from the bottom of the backbone and $6\frac{3}{4}$ in. from the bottom end of the cane. Use fine strong string for tying the cane. The depth of that part of the curve which extends beyond the backbone is about $7\frac{1}{2}$ in. at its centre. Attach the cane, C, in the same way.

Mark the centre of the backbone with a pencil. Lay the ruler on the mark in a horizontal position, and make corresponding marks on the canes. The secondary curves, D and E, are formed from 8 mm. centre cane, split for preference like the canes B and C. They are 2 ft. $8\frac{1}{2}$ in. in length. Glue, bind round and tie D to the bottom end of the main wing cane, C. Bring the cane, D, up in a curve to a point on the backbone, which is $1\frac{1}{2}$ in. below the centre mark and 1 ft. 4 in. from the top end of the cane. Fasten the cane to the backbone at this point. The cane, E, is

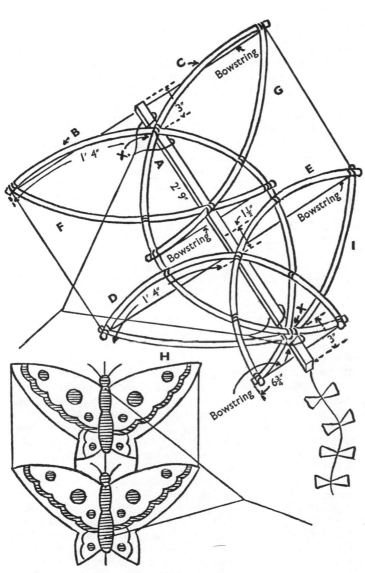

FIG. 15. Double butterfly

tied to the bottom of the main wing cane B, and brought up in a curve to cross over D on the backbone, to which it is securely bound. Continuing the curves on both the canes, bring them to points which are ⅜ in. below the pencil marks on the canes B and C.

The canes F and G are formed from 5 mm. centre cane. They are each 2 ft. 4½ in. in length. Tie F to the top end of B, and bring it in a curve and under C, to a point which is 1½ in. above the centre mark on the backbone, where it is glued, bound round and tied. G is fastened to the top end of C, and, bringing it in a curve over B, is secured at the point where F crosses the backbone. The ends of these two canes F and G are tied at points which are ⅜ in. above the pencil marks on B and C.

Next, add the canes, H and I. These are cut from 5 mm. centre cane and are each 1 ft. 7 in. in length. Bind them to the top ends of D and E. Bring H in a curve, under E and over B, to the bottom joint on the backbone, and tie it at this place. Bring I, under D and C, to the same joint, and tie. All tying points are shown in Fig. 15. It is a good thing to flatten the canes slightly with a sharp knife at these tying points, so that they will hold better. Smear the binding also with thin glue to keep them in position. Before proceeding any farther, inspect the framework to make sure that all the curves match on each side of the backbone.

The framework now has to be curved to a bow shape. This is achieved by firm but gentle pressure of the hands, and by means of bowstrings. These strings are tied to the ends of the framework (see Fig. 15). They tie underneath and clear of the backbone. The depth of the curve at the top of the wings, measuring from the centre of the bowstrings is 2 in. The smaller bowstrings are added to maintain the bow shape. Bracing strings are added as in Fig. 15. These help to distribute the strain which is imposed when the kite is in flight.

Cover the framework with unbleached greaseproof paper, which is obtained in sheets measuring 20 in. × 30 in. Two sheets will be needed. Lay the framework on these and carefully mark out the required shape with a pencil. Allow a margin of 2 in. all round and cut out. Cut slits in the margin to facilitate the work of gluing it to the frame. The reader may find it easier to make the cover before the framework is bowed. Cut two bodies for the butterflies from thin cardboard, each 1 ft. 2 in. in length. Refer to Fig. 15 for the single butterfly kite, for the shape of these. Now decorate the covers, using lacquer which is sold for general painting purposes. A suggested design is shown (Fig. 15), and the colour scheme could be a medium blue background and black bodies with gold or silver spots and wavy bands. Alternatively, the spots and bands could be cut from metal foil and glued on, so that they would reflect the light.

Glue the covers to the framework, the margins overlapping the canes. Glue the bodies in position. Four pipe cleaners are fixed to the backbone to stick out above the heads. A tail about 6 ft. 6 in. in length is required, which is tied to the bottom of the backbone.

The bridle is 5 ft. 6 in. in length. Use strong string and attach it to the backbone in the form of a loop, at the points marked X. Fig. 15 shows where and how the bridle is fastened in order to take advantage of the strength provided by the backbone joints. The cover is pierced in order to thread the bridle string through. Glue small thin cardboard washers to strengthen the paper, at these points.

The kite line is attached to the bridle with a bowline knot and a reef knot. One last point is to fasten strips of insulating tape over the ends of the framework. These act as shock absorbers in the event of the kite being brought swiftly down to the ground.

THE GLIDER KITE

This kite when it is in the air, bears a striking resemblance to a glider. The fact that it is bow shaped in two directions means that a considerable degree of stability can be expected. In the absence of a tail a device is fitted which will help in directional steadiness. The wing, tail, and body, by themselves, do not provide a large sail or cover area, which is helpful in securing buoyancy and lift. To remedy this, an additional cover area is provided in the form of transparent polythene pieces, which assist in the flight of the kite, but do not obscure its distinctive shape.

The first stage is to make the framework (Fig. 16). Cut the backbone A, 2 ft. 6 in. in length from stripwood, $\frac{3}{8}$ in. square. Make shallow grooves at the ends. Drill two holes at points which are $\frac{3}{8}$ in. from each end, and one hole through the sides, which is $\frac{3}{4}$ in. from the top end. The backbone is shaped to a slight curve. In order to do this, first soak the wood in water for an hour and

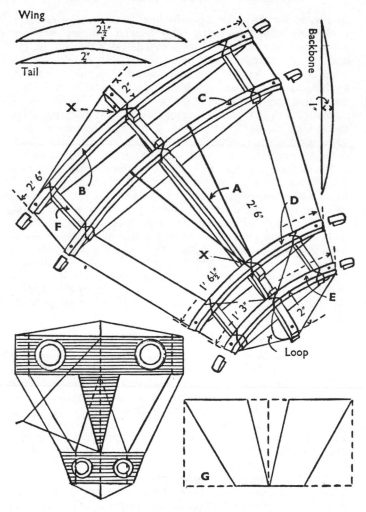

Wing

Tail

Backbone

FIG. 16. Glider

assist the shaping by the application of steam heat. The most convenient method is to lay the wood across a pan of hot water. Following this, the backbone may be readily bent into shape. The shape is retained by means of a bowstring threaded through the holes, $\frac{3}{8}$ in. from the ends, pulled taut and tied securely. The depth of the curve at the centre is 1 in. Set the backbone on one side for a while for the wood to dry out.

Next, cut the crossbars, B and C, which are 2 ft. 6 in. in length. Use split cane, about $\frac{1}{4}$ in. thick. Make shallow grooves in the ends, and also drill holes which are $\frac{1}{2}$ in. from each end. These must now be bowed. To do this, whilst the shaping is in progress, subject the cane to dry heat, by holding it over a gas jet or electric fire. This will prevent cracking and splitting and facilitate the shaping. The depth of the curves at the centre is $2\frac{1}{2}$ in. The shape is retained by means of bowstrings as in the case of the backbone. Lay one crossbar on the other to check that the curves are the same, and make sure that the bowstrings are equally taut.

Now prepare the tail unit, D and E. D is 1 ft. $6\frac{1}{2}$ in. in length, and E is 1 ft. 3 in. Use split cane, which is about $\frac{1}{4}$ in. thick. Make shallow grooves in the ends, and drill holes in them, $\frac{1}{2}$ in. from each end. The bars are bowed in the manner described, using the dry heat method. The depth of the curves at the centre is about 2 in. Lay these bars on the wing crossbars to check that the curves correspond. Join the wing and tail bars together in pairs by means of struts, F. The struts for the wing are 6 in. in length, and those for the tail are 5 in. and all are cut from $\frac{1}{8}$ in. $\times$ $\frac{1}{4}$ in. strip-wood. The wing connecting struts are fixed 2 in. from the ends of the crossbars; the tail struts are fixed 3 in. from the ends of the crossbar D, and 1 in. from the ends of E. Bind them all securely in place on the underside of the crossbars.

Attach the wing and the tail units; the wing at a position where the top crossbar is 2 in. from the end of the backbone; and the tail where its bottom crossbar is 2 in. from the bottom end of the backbone. Glue small stripwood blocks to the backbone on the inside of the wing and the tail frame. Bind round these and the joints with fine string. Smear the binding with thin glue for stiffening. Note that the bow strings lie clear of the backbone on the underside of the framework.

Brace the framework with thin strong string. Thread a length through the hole which is $\frac{3}{4}$ in. from the top end of the backbone, and bind round and tie, leaving a 5 in. tail to the knot. Pass the string over the end of the backbone, and in turn, over the ends of the crossbars and bottom end of the backbone. Finish by bringing the string again over the top end of the backbone, and tie at the first knot. Secure the string in the grooves by means of cloth strips, glued over the ends of the framework.

Secondary bracing strings are added as follows. Tie a length at the bottom left-hand wing joint. Bring it down, loop round and tie at the top left-hand tail joint. Take it to the bottom wing-backbone joint, bind round and tie. From there take the string to the top right-hand tail joint, loop round and tie. Finish by binding round and tying at the bottom right-hand wing joint.

Now tie a length on the bottom left-hand wing crossbar, 3 in. from the backbone. Bring it down to the top tail-backbone joint, loop it round the backbone, and then take it to its tying point on the bottom right-hand wing crossbar, 3 in. from the backbone. See Fig. 16 for details of the bracing. There should be an even tension on all the strings. The wing and tail units should be in the correct horizontal position, and the backbone in the correct vertical position. All the joints must be neat and strongly made.

The framework may now be covered. Use pure ribbed kraft (16 lb.) paper for the wing, body, and tail. Cut a piece first for the body. This is 1 ft. 4 in. in length. The width at the top is 7 in., narrowing to $\frac{1}{2}$ in. at the bottom. Glue this to the bottom wing and the top tail crossbars, and over the body bracing strings, which are shaped like a narrow V. The wing cover measures 2 ft. 8 in. in length and 9 in. in width. Glue it to the crossbars and around the end bracing strings. The tail cover is 8 in. in width, and 1 ft. 8$\frac{1}{2}$ in. in length at the top, narrowing to 1 ft. 5 in. at the bottom. Attach it in the same manner as the wing cover.

There may be added to the main covers a supplementary transparent polythene cover which fills in the spaces between the wing, body, and tail. Use very fine polythene and cut two pieces measuring 1 ft. 4 in. in length and 1 ft. 1$\frac{1}{2}$ in. in width. The shape is given at G (Fig. 16). Secure these to the wing and tail, sides of the body and over the outer bracing strings with strips of cellulose adhesive tape, or one of the proprietary brands of adhesive. Add suitable wing and tail markings, cut from coloured gummed paper.

The bridle is formed from a 6 ft. length of stout string. It is attached to the backbone in the form of a loop at the points marked X (Fig. 16). The kite line is fastened to the bridle with a bowline knot and a reef knot. See Chapter 7, under 'Knots', for details of these.

Next form a loop of string between the bottom tail crossbar and the bottom of the backbone. Tie one end in a bow, so that it can easily be undone. Cut thin washers from cotton reels, which may be threaded on the loop. This device is fitted in place of a tail. One or more of the washers can be suspended by the loop if the kite approaches too near the horizontal in flight. Acting like a weight on a pair of scales, the washers will tilt the nose of the kite upwards. If desired, a windmill may be attached to the top of the backbone. Instructions for making one are given in Chapter 7, under 'Accessories'.

CHAPTER SIX

Sail: Wing: Box: Smiling Face

THE SAIL KITE

THIS kite shows the influence of the box kite in its structure. It is in two parts; one being in the form of a triangle; the other in the form of a sail. It is designed to achieve steady flight in different weather conditions, and should be capable of attaining to a good height quickly. It is robust in construction to withstand the normal wear and tear of flying and handling.

The first stage is to make the crossbars, A and B. They are formed from ¼ in. square stripwood. A is 2 ft. 6 in. in length, and B is 1 ft. 8 in. The ends are grooved, as shown at C (Fig. 17). Next, make the two longerons, D and E. These are each 2 ft. 6 in. in length, and are cut from stripwood, ⅜ in. square. Groove them at the ends, as at C.

Assemble the four pieces to form a framework. Lay the longerons on top of the crossbars, and join together with glue and ¾ in. fretwork nails. Bend the ends of these over and hammer flat. Before nailing, part drill through the wood to prevent it splitting. Inject a little light machine oil into the holes as a further safeguard. See Fig. 17 for the measurements relating to the assembly of the framework. Now bind round the joints with fine string. This frame must be really firm, so that it will keep its correct shape in flight.

Proceed by making the triangular framework. A third longeron, F, which is 2 ft. 6 in. in length is cut from ¼ in. square stripwood. Two upright struts, G and H, are also needed. Cut them from ¼ in. square stripwood, and make them 9⅞ in. in length. Cut a V-shaped groove at one end of each, to a depth of ⅛ in. to act as a cradle for the top longeron. Bind round the struts with strong thread just below the V-shapes. This will prevent them splitting during flight. Now smooth every part with fine sandpaper, and apply a coat of clear varnish, after which the frame pieces may be enamelled, if desired.

Next, brace the sail frame. Bind round and tie a length of fine string to the right-hand end of the top crossbar, leaving a 5 in. tail

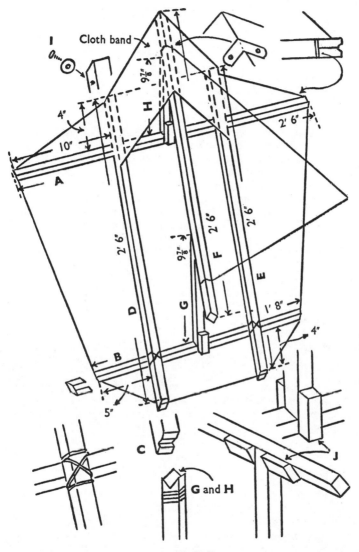

FIG. 17. Sail

where it is knotted. Take the string round the edges of the frame to form an outline for the sail. Complete the bracing by tying to the tail at the first knot. The bracing must be taut in order to provide a firm support for the sail. When you are satisfied that this has been achieved, stick strips of insulating tape over the ends of the frame. They will keep the string in place and prevent the wood from splitting.

Use cambric or very fine calico for the sail. Pin the material to a board. Lay the framework upon it, and with a soft-grade pencil, mark the shape. Add a margin of 1 in. all round. The cover may be decorated at this stage. Use fabric painting oil colours. The design should be simple and bold, for example, it might be a large centre circle or diamond-shape, with the surround edged with the same colour; or one's initials, in the form of a monogram could be painted on. When the paint is dry, cut out the cover.

The method of securing the cover to its frame is as follows. Roll the material on to a 3 ft. length of $\frac{1}{2}$ in. diameter dowelling. By doing this, the cover can be stretched evenly as it is being attached. Fasten the cover to the top of the two longerons, D and E, by means of fretwork nails. Place small cardboard strips between the material and the nail heads. Roll the cover down and fasten in the same way to the ends of the top crossbar. Next, keeping it as firmly stretched as possible, fasten at the ends of the bottom crossbar, and lastly, to the bottom ends of the longerons. A better way, instead of using nails, would be to use $\frac{1}{4}$ in. round-headed fine brass screws, with small washers, which may be cut from tin or obtained from model-makers' shops. Drill holes part way through the wood to receive the screws, as one would also do for nails. Now fold the margin over the bracing strings and sew down. The cover may be further secured by the use of a few extra nails or screws along the crossbars. No more than two or three should be used, as too many will tend to weaken the crossbars. The result should be an evenly stretched, firmly secured and well-balanced sail.

The next stage is to complete the triangular shape. Two cloth bands, as at I (Fig. 17) are needed. Cut two pieces, $22\frac{3}{4}$ in. in length and 9 in. in width. Fold over $\frac{1}{2}$ in. of the material all round, make a crease at the folds and sew down to make a hem. Now make a sharp crease along the centre of the bands, going across the width of the material. Fasten the bands at these creases to the third longeron, so that one edge of this fits into the creases. Secure the longeron in this position with glue, and a nail or screw at each end of the bands. Now attach the free ends of the bands to the ends of the longerons D and E. Use glue, and for preference ¼ in. fine brass screws with washers. About four will be needed for each end of the covers. Instead of washers one may use thin tin strips which are 8 in. in length and ¼ in. in width.

Take the two upright struts, G and H, and insert them between the top longeron and the crossbars. They must be a good fit, otherwise the cloth bands will be too slack. They are 9⅞ in. in length, as has been previously stated, but it is a good thing to cut them slightly oversize, so that they can be trimmed to the length required, which may vary from the one given. As these struts are subjected to considerable strain in flight, they must be reinforced with small glued blocks, fixed in the position shown at J (Fig. 17). Both struts will need six blocks, 1 in. × ¼ in. square.

The bridle is made from stout string, 6 ft. in length. Tie it in the form of a loop to the top longeron, 4 in. from each end. In order to do this, the bands must be pierced, and they will need strengthening at these points with strips of material, glued in place. The kite line is attached to the bridle by means of a bowline knot and a reef knot, see Chapter 7, under 'Knots', for details of these. These kites do not need a tail, and balance is improved by the correct position of the line on the bridle which is found by experiment whilst flying the kite. When this has been found, the kite will climb and soar in a most satisfactory manner.

THE WING KITE

Robust construction and pleasing design are combined in the wing kite. Because it carries a comparatively large area of framework, which results in increased weight, it may be found to fly best in a fresh to strong wind. However, in practised hands this kite proves to be quite versatile in flight.

Begin by forming the main framework. Cut four crossbars for the wings, A, B, C, and D. Each measures 2 ft. 6 in. in length. Use ¼ in. square stripwood. Make grooves in each end. Cut two longerons from ⅜ in. sq. stripwood, 2 ft. 8 in. in length, which are also grooved at the ends. See E and F (Fig. 18). The longerons are glued and nailed to the crossbars at the positions shown in

C

Fig. 18. Use ¾ in. fretwork nails. Bend the ends over and hammer them flat. Part drill through the wood to receive the nails and put a spot of oil in the holes. Add eight wooden blocks in the positions indicated. They are cut from ¼ in. square stripwood and are 1 in. in length. Fix them with glue and nails. A third longeron, G, and four upright struts, H, I, J, and K, are made at this stage, but are assembled later on; ¼ in. square stripwood is used. The longeron is 2 ft. 8 in. in length and is not grooved at the ends. The struts measure 9⅞ in. and at one end are cut in a V shape, which is ⅛ in. in depth. Smooth all parts thoroughly with fine sandpaper. Apply a coat of clear varnish and set aside to dry.

Following this, the framework is braced with thin strong string. Make a start by binding it round and tying it to the right-hand end of the top crossbar, leaving a 4 in. free length beyond the knot. From there take it round the ends of the framework, by means of the grooves provided. Return to where you started and knot the ends together securely. As a safeguard against possible distortion of the framework whilst this work is being done, use the following device. Take two 2 ft. 6 in. lengths of stripwood and bind them near the ends of the crossbars. These are removed when the bracing is completed. Glue strips of material over the ends of the framework to keep the bracing in place

Cover the framework with cambric or fine calico to make the wings. Two pieces are needed, measuring 2 ft. 7 in. in length and 11 in. in width. This allows for ½ in. margin all round. Fold the margin over, iron it flat and sew down to make a hem. If desired the pieces may now be decorated. See Chapter 7, 'Accessories', for suggested designs. Secure these pieces to the crossbars. Use glue and ¼ in. round-headed fine brass screws with small washers. The cloth should be stretched as tightly as possible, but do not bend the crossbars. Use temporary stripwood supports, and insert between the ends of the crossbars, to keep them in shape.

Complete the triangular part of the kite. Make first the two cloth bands, of which only one, M, is shown (Fig. 18). They are of the same material as the wings and measure 23½ in. in length and 11 in. in width, this providing for a ½ in. margin which forms a hem all round as described above. Any decoration should now be added. Form a crease at the centre of each to show where to glue and nail the third longeron, G. The bands are fitted 1 in.

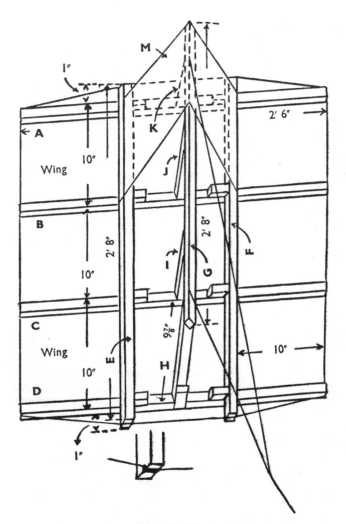

FIG. 18. Wing

from each end of this. Attach the bands to the other longerons with glue and $\frac{1}{4}$ in. screws and washers.

The next step is to insert the upright struts. They are glued and nailed to the centre of the crossbars and to the top longeron. They must keep the bands as taut as possible without distorting the framework. Cut them oversize and then trim them to ensure a good fit. Strengthen the two end struts with small glued blocks, cut from $\frac{1}{4}$ in. square stripwood. Two will be required for each strut.

A 5 ft. 6 in. length of strong string is used for the bridle. It is tied to the top longeron in the form of a loop. In order to do this, pierce the cloth bands, 5 in. from each end, and reinforce them at these points with strips of glued material.

The kite string is attached to the bridle by means of a bowline knot and a reef knot. See Chapter 7, under 'Knots', for details of these.

As an additional decoration, paper fringes may be glued to the bracing between the wings.

THE BOX KITE

This is probably the best known and most popular of all kites. It is an excellent flyer, and is made to withstand rough weather. No difficulty will be met with in constructing one, if the instructions are followed carefully.

The four corner pieces, called longerons, A, B, C, D, are formed from stripwood, or other wood which can be cut to size. They are $\frac{3}{8}$ in. square and 3 ft. 6 in. in length, and should be straight, smooth and free from knots. It is advisable to give them a coat of clear varnish, and then put on one side to dry.

The four diagonal struts are approximately 2 ft. 1 in. in length, E and F. They can be made from either $\frac{1}{4}$ in. × $\frac{1}{2}$ in. stripwood, or plywood. These, too, should be varnished. They are cut somewhat longer than the actual measurement. When the kite is being assembled, they can be trimmed to give a really tight fit. This will ensure something which is really essential—firm cloth bands.

Two cloth bands are required, of which one, G, is shown in Fig. 19. In the illustration, the front band has been removed, so that details of the framework may be seen more clearly. The bands

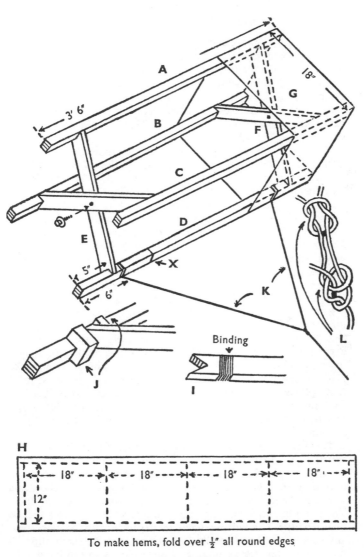

A

3' 6"

B

C

D

E

5"

6"

X

F

G

18"

J

Binding

I

K

L

H

18"   18"   18"   18"

12"

To make hems, fold over ½" all round edges

FIG. 19. Box

are made from lightweight material, which at the same time must be strong. Cambric or fine calico is recommended. Each measures 6 ft. 1 in. in length and 1 ft. 1 in. in width. Form a hem along the two long sides, for which $\frac{1}{2}$ in. turning has been allowed. Sew the two long sides first. Then make a $\frac{1}{2}$ in. turn along the two short ends, and oversew together. You have now two endless bands, each measuring 6 ft. × 1 ft. They should be free from wrinkles (see Fig. 19, H).

The next stage is to lay them flat on the table, and with a hot iron, smooth them out, making creases at the folds. Fold them over again, and repeat the action with the iron. The bands will now have four creases, at intervals of 18 in. These indicate the position of the longerons. Place the first longeron along the crease made at the oversewn ends of the band. Fasten together with $\frac{3}{8}$ in. fine brass screws. Repeat the process with the other longerons, one edge of each fitting snugly into the crease provided. Care must be taken in assembling the bands. Do not wrinkle or tear the material.

Now take one of the diagonal struts. Mark the exact centre. Drill through with a $\frac{1}{8}$ in. diameter bit. Place this strut on top of a second, and join them together with a fine-gauge screw. The diameter of the hole is slightly larger than that of the screw, to enable the two struts to open and close freely. Care is needed to avoid splitting the wood. To help prevent this, apply a little light machine oil at the spots where the drilling and screwing take place. The ends of the struts are cut V-shaped, as shown at I (Fig. 19), and are bound round with strong thread, to prevent splitting, when the kite is assembled. Apply a little glue where you bind the strut. This will keep the thread permanently in position.

The best method of inserting the struts is as follows. Get someone to open the kite out, stand it on end, and hold it squarely in place. This will enable you to slide the struts down until they are 5 in. from the ends of the longerons. As the struts were cut slightly oversize, it might be necessary to trim the ends. The thing to aim at is, that when the struts are fixed they will be bowed a little. This will exert maximum pressure on the longerons, and so keep the bands really taut. To prevent the struts slipping out of position, secure small L-shaped blocks to the longerons. Use glue and one fine panel pin for each block (see Fig. 19, J).

The bridle is fastened to one of the longerons in the form of a loop, K. It is 6 in. from either end. Use really strong string. A piece 7 ft. 6 in. in length will be required. In attaching the bridle it is necessary to pierce the bands. In order to strengthen them at these points, glue strips of material to the bands, thus providing a double thickness. The stiffening supplied by the glued strip will prevent tears and fraying.

The kite line is attached to the bridle by means of a reef knot and a bowline knot. The method of tying these is shown in Fig. 19, L. In this way the kite line can be adjusted on the bridle, to suit varying weather conditions. Generally speaking, such adjustments mean that the lighter the wind, the shorter the front line of the bridle will be. In a very strong wind, it might be necessary to tie the kite line directly to the longeron, just behind the front band. This would be at the point marked X. It must be emphasized that a really strong kite line is needed. It must be capable of withstanding considerable strain. Do not be tempted to use string of inferior quality. The price usually paid for this is a lost kite.

The appearance of the kite is enhanced if the wooden framework is enamelled in suitable colours. In addition, designs could be painted on the bands. Students' oil colours may be used. A choice of designs is given in Chapter 7. This work would have to be done, of course, before the kite was assembled.

Smiling Face

This kite is formed after the pattern of the Pegtop kite and if made properly should prove to be a good flyer.

The backbone, A, is formed from $\frac{3}{8}$ in. $\times$ $\frac{1}{4}$ in. stripwood and it is 3 ft. in length and grooved at the bottom end. It should be straight and free from knots and cracks. The crossbar, B, is formed from $\frac{1}{4}$ in. square stripwood and is 2 ft. in length. This is joined to the backbone 9 in. from the top, by means of glue and fine string.

The bow, C, requires split cane, about $\frac{1}{4}$ in. thick, which is about 2 ft. 9 in. in length. This is curved to the shape shown (Fig. 20). The shaping is made easier if the cane is subjected to dry heat, such as a gas jet or an electric fire. The bow shape is retained by means of a string which is bound securely to the ends of the cane.

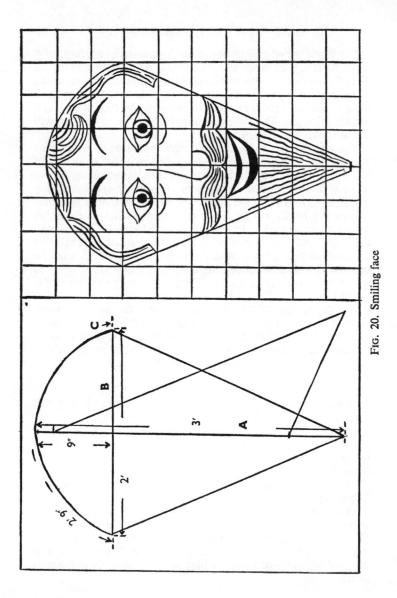

FIG. 20. Smiling face

Bind the centre of the bow to the top of the backbone, and the ends of the bow to the ends of the crossbar. Now take a strong bracing string from one end of the bow, pass it over the bottom end of the backbone, and then up to the other end of the bow.

The cover is made from cambric or very fine calico. The method of preparing is as follows. First draw a grid of 4 in. squares on a sheet of paper and then copy on to it the face shown in Fig. 20. Next, pin the cover material to a board and transfer the face to it by means of carbon paper. Hold the paper pattern down with cellulose tape or drawing pins while this is being done. Then paint the face with fabric painting oil colours. When these have dried, cut out the shape, allowing a margin of $1\frac{1}{2}$ in. all round.

The cover is fitted by folding the margin over the curved cane and the bracing string and sewing down. Keep it as well stretched as possible.

The bridle is attached in the form of a loop. Use strong string about 7 ft. in length and tie it at points which are 9 in. from the bottom and $3\frac{1}{2}$ in. from the top of the backbone. The cover must be pierced to do this. Glue cloth washers around the holes to strengthen the material at these points. Attach the kite line to the bridle by means of a bowline knot and a reef knot. A tail about 7 ft. in length is fitted. Tie the tail papers about 9 in. apart from one another.

CHAPTER SEVEN

Tools, materials, methods, accessories

THIS chapter is concerned with the hows, whys and wherefores of the things which are used in kite making and flying. We begin with a few words about tools, of which the following are recommended.

TOOLS

First, a fretsaw, for cutting the small joints which are sometimes used. Second, a small hacksaw, or a small tenon saw, for cutting lengths of wood. Third, for a hammer, use what is called a pin hammer. Other tools include a craft knife with spare blades; a small screwdriver; a small file; a hand drill, with bits up to $\frac{1}{8}$ in. diameter; a fretsaw drill or an awl for making nail and screw holes; a small brad punch to drive nails home; a rule; a pair of scissors; a soft-grade pencil; a few assorted paintbrushes. In addition, a woodworker's vice comes in handy, as also do one or two cramps for holding down glued joints.

MATERIALS

In considering the various materials which are used we come first to wood for the framework. It is possible to make a kite from odd scraps of wood, or even hedgerow sticks, but in the long run it pays to use the best. The wood must meet with certain requirements, namely; it must be light in weight, smooth, strong, and flexible. Fortunately, this kind is readily obtained in the form of hardwood stripwood. It can be obtained at woodworkers' and model-makers' shops. It comes in lengths up to 8 ft. and is of different thicknesses. When you are buying wood it is a good thing to tell the shopkeeper what you want it for, and he will help you in the choice. This stripwood is most suitable for the purpose, because besides being light and strong it is also fairly flexible, though not to the same extent, of course, as cane.

Cane is often specified in kite making, generally for the cross-bars when these have to be bowed. That which is generally referred to is known as gardener's or staking cane. The hard outer skin gives great strength and flexibility to small diameter lengths. It is supplied both in the form of whole cane and split cane. Of course, one may split the cane at home when necessary by using a sharp knife or fretsaw.

Other cane mentioned in this book is called centre cane. It is cut from rattan, a species of climbing palm belonging to the East Indies. The hard outer skin of the rattan is stripped off, leaving the centre cane. It provides lengths of uniform thickness, but, however, it does not possess the strength of whole cane, as it lacks the hard outer skin. It may be used in suitable diameters when difficult shaping is called for, as it may be easily worked. Handicraft stores usually stock centre cane.

Covers for kites can be made in several materials. The most common is tissue paper. It is chosen mainly because of its lightness, but it is flimsy stuff and must be handled with care. Sheets of the paper measure 20 in. × 30 in., and various colours may be obtained. Following correspondence with a well-known paper manufacturers, and after testing, the writer recommends the following as being superior to tissue paper: *one*, pure unbleached greaseproof (17/18 lb.); *two*, mg. pure ribbed kraft (16 lb.). Both are light in weight and very strong. A good quality adhesive should be used for gluing the greaseproof. Both papers are obtainable in sheets measuring 20 in. × 30 in. A cloth cover is specified for some kites. This may be made of fine smooth silk, very fine calico or cambric. The usual width of these is 36 in.

The right kind of glue is an important factor in kite making, since the joints must be of the maximum strength. Generally speaking, glues are divided into the synthetic; the animal, and the fish glues. The two latter, when properly used, are very strong. They are gap-fillers in joints which do not fit too well. Another advantage is that they do not deteriorate so quickly in the tin or tube as do some other types. 'Croid' or 'Seccotine' are especially recommended.

The cellulose cements are very much to the fore in the synthetic adhesives. They are widely-known as 'balsa cements' and are used for their strength and quick-setting properties. Unless they are properly sealed when not in use, they have a tendency to harden. As a general rule, the quicker in setting the cement is, the shorter is the time that it will keep in a working condition, particularly when once the container has been opened. Most kinds of cellulose adhesives are suitable for balsa wood, paper, and card, but for ordinary wood a slower drying kind is needed. This is known as 'high strength' balsa cement.

Mention may also be made of an adhesive derived from polyvinyl acetate (p.v.a.). This is an excellent general purpose glue. It is quick-setting and very strong, and provides slightly flexible joints. It is non-staining and therefore is a good choice where cloth covers are glued and not sewn down.

The synthetic resin glues, of which there are many, make up another great group. They give great joint strength, and are waterproof. Certain proprietary brands are supplied with the resin and hardener ready mixed, requiring only the addition of water.

String comes next in the list of materials. This is the general name for the material used for the bracing, bridle, tail, and kite line. The string is required in different strengths and thicknesses according to the purpose it serves, and the size of the kite. The writer, after consultation with a manufacturer, and after many tests, recommends the following as being suitable for the kites listed in the book.

In the case of the larger kites, up to 3 ft. 6 in. in length, use fine flax line for the bracing, and No. 68 hemp whipcord for the bridle and the kite line. Flax line may also be used for the tail. The line is available in knots of 17–20 yards. For the smaller kites and to serve a general purpose, use No. 10 or 104 coloured cotton, or linen tent thread. These should serve for kites up to say, 2 ft. in length.

The appearance of a kite is improved when it is decorated in some way. A few simple designs are given later in the chapter. These may be cut from coloured gummed paper, or painted directly on to the kite cover. Use fabric painting oil colours for cloth covers. Lacquer is most suitable for paper covers. It spreads easily, gives a clear-cut outline and dries fairly quickly.

METHODS

Joints

The simple butt joint is all that is generally needed in kite making. It may be formed in two ways: first, by laying one piece of wood across another, and fastening together with glue and binding thread; second, by fastening two ends together with glue and a nail. When properly made, the butt joint combines simplicity with strength.

The halving joint is used to make a framework all on one level, that is, one part does not stick out above or below another. This makes for neatness, and enables the kite cover to lie flat upon all the framework. This joint, to be effective, must be made accurately. A good joint is one in which the parts need a gentle tapping home with a mallet. Both these joints are described and illustrated in the instructions for making kites in Chapters 1-6.

Gluing

When using glue, first read the directions on the container. It is surprising how many people don't do this, and then blame the glue because it won't stick. These directions usually state the approximate drying time, that is, the time to be allowed before the parts are brought together. Drying time is fundamental to successful gluing.

Don't use too much glue. Too much is nearly as useless as none at all, and far messier. After they have been set aside for a while to dry, the two parts are pressed firmly together. The ultimate strength of the joint depends upon the closeness of contact of the two pieces of wood. The aim is to expel all air bubbles, which are the enemy of good joints. The work is best done in a fairly warm room. It is an advantage to cramp the joints and to allow the glue to set hard overnight. Metal cramps can be bought quite cheaply.

Binding

In addition to the use of glue, most kite framework joints are bound round with thread or fine string. Use thread for small kites and fine string for the larger sizes. Smear the binding with glue to keep it in place. Illustrations in Chapters 1-6 will show how to achieve neat and effective binding of joints.

Shaping Wood and Cane

We will take wood first. When the framework is to be bowed and suitable cane cannot be obtained, it is possible to shape hardwood stripwood. Many kinds of wood may be shaped by steaming. Professional woodworkers use a steaming box; but as an alternative, the wood may be soaked for a minute or two in warm water, and then laid across a pan of hot water. It should, after a while, be sufficiently pliable to be formed, gently but firmly, into the required shape, which shape should be fixed by the use of a bowstring. The shaping should be done before the parts are glued and assembled.

Cane, being naturally flexible, is readily formed into curves. Whole or split cane is more easily bent by the application of dry heat (e.g. gas jet, or electric fire). This method prevents cracking or splitting. Again, in the case of kite crossbars, the shape is retained by the immediate use of bowstrings. Other shaped parts should be fixed in position as soon as possible.

Centre cane, which may be used when small sharp curves have to be made, is rendered more pliable by soaking it in hot or cold water. After the parts have been shaped, strings can be run across the ends to prevent the cane from springing back while it dries out.

Cane may be cut, split, and drilled quite easily. The best way of cutting it is to use the knife so that it rolls the cane round at the same time as it is cutting through it. This will prevent the ends from splintering. Cane can be split with a sharp-pointed knife. Don't use it as though it were a chisel, but draw it firmly, using the point, along the cane. It will be necessary to repeat the action in order to separate the cane. Nodes or knots are best cut through with a fretsaw. It is a good plan to drill through the cane near the ends, and pin it to a board. This will prevent the cane from rolling while the splitting is being done. When drilling cane, care must be taken not to split it. As soon as the drill pierces the underside, turn it over and drill through again.

KNOTS AND HITCHES

The difference between a knot and a hitch is that a knot makes a more lasting fastening. Again, a knot may be formed on the string itself, whereas a hitch usually requires some other object to which it can be attached. There are various knots and hitches, and from among them a few have been chosen as being useful in kite making and flying.

1. Most knots are formed from a loop or bight, A. The parts

belonging to it are, the standing part, B, and the end, C. (Fig. 21).

2. *Overhand knot.* This is the simplest to make and forms a part of many other knots. It is the one used for knotting the sewing thread when a cloth cover is required for a kite. It may also serve, when repeated once or twice, for tying the bracing strings (Fig. 21).

3. *Reef knot.* Known also as the square knot and the sailor's knot, it is undoubtedly the simplest and best with which to fasten together two strings of equal thickness. It is chosen, along with the bowline knot, for attaching the kite line to the bridle (Fig. 21).

4. *Bowline knot.* This is called the king of knots. It is so called because of its general usefulness and reliability. Fig. 21 shows the correct way of forming it.

5. *Clove hitch.* It may be said that this is the best known hitch, being widely used because it is easy to form, and is very reliable. The stronger the pull against it, the firmer it holds. It may be used for fastening the paper pieces to the tail string and for similar attachments. A and B (Fig. 21) show the stages in forming the hitch.

6. *Clove hitch slip knot.* Because it forms what is called a running noose, it is recommended when one wishes to secure the kite line temporarily to a post or other anchor whilst the kite is in flight (Fig. 21).

7. *Fisherman's bend.* When there is a varying strain on the string, this will prove to be most reliable. It may therefore be used for tying bracing strings and bowstrings. When it is correctly formed, it may be readily untied in order to make any necessary adjustments of the strings (Fig. 21).

The reader is advised to practise making these knots and hitches so that they may be quickly and properly formed.

ACCESSORIES

In this section there will be found instructions and illustrations for making a number of things which add to the enjoyment of kite flying.

Reel

A reel or winder may be regarded as a necessity. It is not merely something upon which the line is wound. If the line is thought of as being the 'motor', then obviously the reel assists it in its

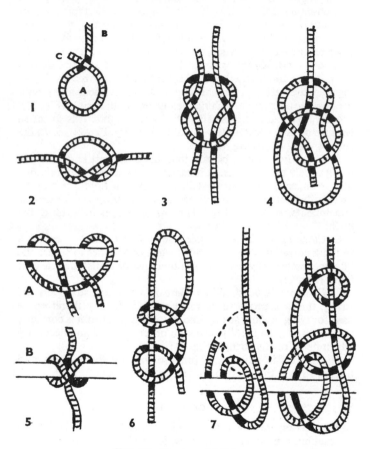

FIG. 21. Knots and hitches

PLATE I. Voisin Biplane, 1908–9, showing the influence of the box-kite in its structure

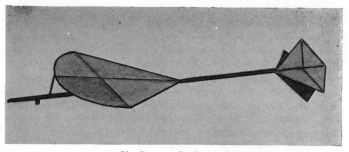

PLATE II. Sir George Cayley's glider, 1804

PLATE III. Boy flying kite (c.1600)

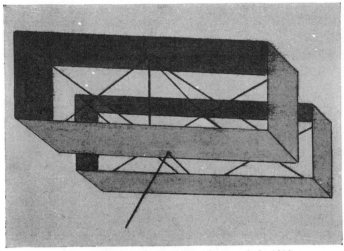

PLATE IV. Hargrave box-kite, first made in 1893

PLATE V An early reproduction illustrating a Chinese man and child flying kites

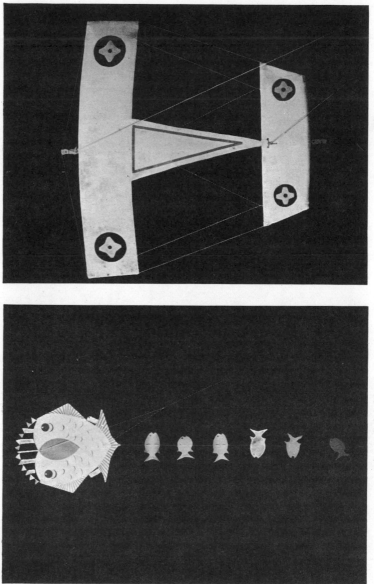

PLATE VI. A small fish kite

PLATE VII. A glider kite

important function. Obviously, the size of the reel will be governed by the size of the kite, and the amount and thickness of the line. Therefore the measurements given here may be suited to individual requirements.

The reel shown in Fig. 22 is of a convenient size. As will be seen, it is a revolving spindle type, with a simple locking device, which enables the operator to have a hand free at times to attend to other things.

The reel is made up of eleven separate parts, and is constructed as follows. Cut two 4 in. diameter circles from $\frac{3}{16}$ in. plywood, as at A. Cut $\frac{7}{8}$ in. diameter holes through the centres. The spindle, B, is formed from $\frac{7}{8}$ in. diameter round rod, and measures $6\frac{1}{4}$ in. in length. Cut two side pieces, as at C, measuring 5 in. × $4\frac{1}{8}$ in. Use wood, $\frac{1}{2}$ in. thick.

Drill $\frac{7}{8}$ in. diameter holes through them at the positions shown. Make them slightly over-size, by means of a round file, so that the spindle revolves freely. The base, D, measures 5 in. × $4\frac{1}{8}$ in. and is made from wood, $\frac{1}{2}$ in. thick.

Fit the spindle to the circular pieces. The left-hand piece is glued $\frac{5}{8}$ in. from one end of the spindle; the right-hand piece, $1\frac{1}{4}$ in. from the other end. Attach the side pieces to this unit. Place thin washers on the spindle between these sides and the circular pieces. Next, add the base, D. Use glue and 1 in. fine flat-headed screws, and counter-sink the holes for them. Place the base between the side pieces, otherwise the subsequent measurements will be wrong.

The handle is in two parts, E and F. E measures $3\frac{3}{4}$ in. × 2 in. and is cut from wood which is $\frac{1}{2}$ in. thick. Cut two $\frac{7}{8}$ in. diameter holes, $\frac{1}{2}$ in. from the top and the bottom. Make them slightly under-size, to ensure a good fit for the spindle, and the rod, F, both of which should need tapping home with a mallet. The rod, F, is $4\frac{1}{2}$ in. in length and is cut from $\frac{7}{8}$ in. diameter round rod. Fit it into one of the holes, and secure it with glue and a 1 in. fine screw, which is driven through at the position shown. Now place E on the spindle and make fast with glue and a 1 in. fine screw, the position of which is shown in Fig. 22. Place a thin washer on the spindle between the side piece and the handle.

The bottom handle, G, is 5 in. in length and is cut from $\frac{7}{8}$ in. diameter round rod. Make a small holding block, H. This is 3 in. in length and 2 in. in width. Drill a $\frac{7}{8}$ in. diameter hole through

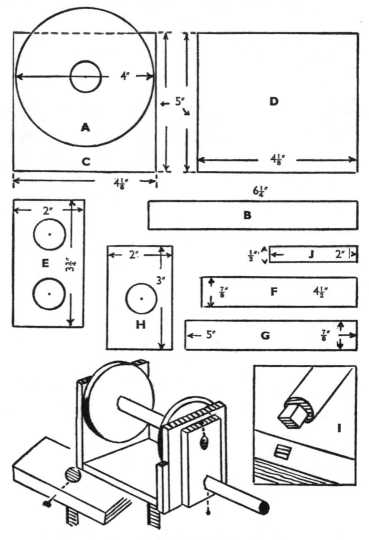

FIG. 22. Kite line reel (No. 1)

the centre, and insert the handle, G. The latter should fit tightly in its hole, so that it requires tapping home with a mallet. Secure with glue and a 1 in. fine screw, which is driven through at the position shown. The holding block is then glued and screwed to the base.

The method of joining the parts by means of a screw has been chosen for its simplicity. Those who prefer it may use the square mortise and tenon joint, as shown at I.

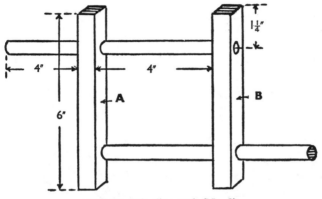

FIG. 23. Kite line reel. (No. 2)

The locking device, J, is a strip of wood, ½ in. thick; or better still, a metal strip. It measures 2 in. × ½ in., and is secured to the side at the position shown, by means of a screw. When it is turned to the horizontal position, it locks the handle.

Sandpaper all parts thoroughly. Apply a coat of size to fill the grain, and when this is dry, enamel in bright colours. In order to ensure the smooth running of the spindle, coat the edges of its holes with blacklead or graphite paste. The things just mentioned are best done before the reel is finally assembled.

A Simpler Type of Reel

This is illustrated in Fig. 23. The upright strips, A and B, are 6 in. in length and are cut from 1 in. square stripwood. Drill two holes, ½ in. in diameter at positions 1 in. from the top and the bottom. Cut two pieces of dowelling, ½ in. diameter and 10 in. in length. These are attached to the upright strips in the manner shown. The ends of the rods form handles, which measure 4 in. in length. Sandpaper all parts thoroughly; apply a coat of size, and when this has dried, finish with enamel.

Parachutes

Fig. 24 illustrates the stages in the making of these. They are easily made, and add to the enjoyment of kite flying. They travel

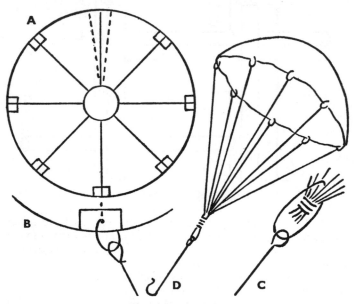

FIG. 24. Parachute

up the kite line, to which a stop block is tied. When they reach the block, a sharp jerk of the line will release them, whereupon they will float gently down to earth.

Cut a circle of tissue paper, 12 in. in diameter. At the centre of this, paste a 1 in. diameter circle of thin cardboard. Cut eight slits in the paper, extending to the cardboard centre-piece, as shown at A. Shape the paper by overlapping the slits to an extent of ⅜ in. at the bottom and narrowing to a point at the centre-piece. Glue cardboard strips, ½ in. square, over the ends of the joints. Pierce small holes in these strips, and insert small loops of thread. To these tie pieces of stout thread, 1 ft. in length, B. Before they are tied, wax the pieces of thread. Use beeswax or a stiff furniture polish. This will stiffen them, and prevent them from getting tangled in flight. Gather their ends together and bind round with cotton. A loop of thread hangs from the binding, as shown at C. A hook is formed from a 6 in. length of wire. The wire must not be too fine, as it provides the weight which keeps the parachute in the right position as it descends. One end of the wire is securely attached to the thread loop; the other end, D, hooks on to the kite line. The parachutes look most attractive when they are made from tissue paper of various colours.

To operate them, first tie a 4 in. strip of ⅜ in. square stripwood to the kite line, a few yards below the kite. This forms the stop block. Now place the parachutes on the line, one at a time. Agitate the line, but not in such a way that the parachutes jump off. The wind will carry them up the line until they reach the stop block, where they are released.

Wind Funnels (Fig. 25)

These may be fitted to plane-type kites. They are obviously decorative, but also serve to supply a light current of air to the kite on a calm day. The air travels through them at increased pressure which improves the kite's upward movement.

To make them, first form a circle of thin wire, 3 in. in diameter, and join the ends together with thread. The wire may be shaped round a tin or a bottle. Next, take a piece of fairly stiff paper, measuring 10 in. × 5 in., and shape it in the following way. Hold it at the bottom corners. Twist the left-hand corner over and downwards. Wrap the other corner over to form a funnel. Cup one hand round the funnel to retain the shape. The funnel may then be adjusted to a diameter of 3½ in. at the top and 1 in. at the bottom. Having done this, apply glue to the overlap and stick down. Now cut the edges straight at the top and bottom, and make slits in the top edge to a depth of ¼ in. Apply glue to this ½ in. margin, fold over the wire rim and press down.

Now add the fringe. Take a piece of tissue paper which is 1 in. square. Fold it down the centre and paste the ends together. Cut ½ in. slits in the paper along the pasted side. This forms the margin. Wrap the paper round the funnel, and mark the overlap, which is then pasted down. Apply paste to the top margin, fold it over

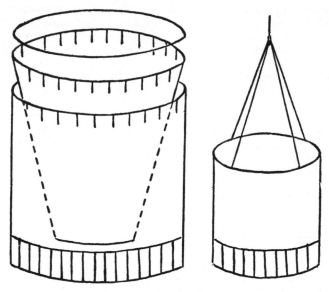

FIG. 25. Balancing funnels

the rim and fasten down. Now cut the tissue paper into fingers, ½ in. in width, to form a fringe.

Next, pierce the top in four places, representing 12, 3, 6 and 9 o'clock positions. Insert thin strings which are 1 ft. 3 in. in length, and form them into loops. Tie the loops together at the top so that there is an equal tension on all of them. Attach the wind funnels to the kite by means of strings, as shown for the 'Star' kite. Please note that the funnels which have been described are intended for kites which are 2 ft. to 2 ft. 6 in. in size. The measurements given may be adapted for larger or smaller kites.

Tassels

These are illustrated in Fig. 26, and are designed to be tied to the end of the kite tail; to the backbone, or to the bottom corners of the framework. The appearance of the 'Festoon' or the 'Tonking' kites is improved by the addition of tassels.

The method of making them is as follows. Cut a circle of tissue paper, 12 in. in diameter. Draw on it an inner circle, which is 3 in. in diameter. Fold the paper into four, as shown at A, with the

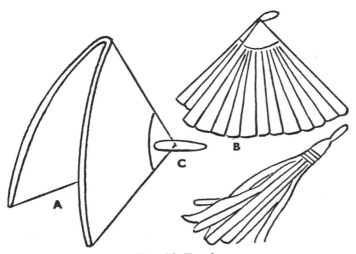

FIG. 26. Tassels

marking for the smaller circle on the outside. Next, cut into fingers which extend to the circumference of the smaller circle, as at B. Take a piece of thin string, 6 in. in length, and tie it in the form of a loop. Glue one end of this to a segment of the inner circle, as at C. Roll the paper round at the top, and bind round with thread. The tassel is now ready to be tied to a trailing string by means of the loop.

Windmill or Whizzer (Fig. 27)

A novel touch is added when one of these is fixed to the top of a kite backbone. The windmill described is suitable for the larger kites; the measurements given may be adapted for smaller ones.

You will need an 8 in. square of fairly stiff but pliable cardboard. Draw lines on it, to divide it into four equal parts, and make a small hole through the centre. Next, draw the pattern on the square, as shown, and cut out the shaded parts.

Following this, bring the corners, A and B, over in curves to the centre. Allow a sufficient amount of the corners to overlap, and fasten them together with glue. Bring C and D together in

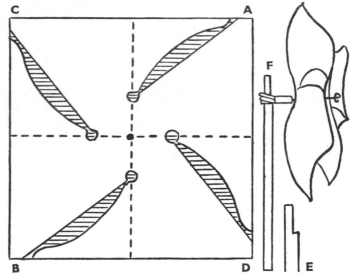

FIG. 27. Windmill

the same way, over A and B. Make a small hole in the glued parts, which will be in line with the first centre hole.

Cut a piece of $\frac{1}{4}$ in. diameter dowelling, $9\frac{1}{2}$ in. in length. Flatten it at the top with a sharp knife, as at E. Take an 8 in. length of thin strong wire, and wrap $3\frac{1}{2}$ in. of this tightly round the flattened part of the dowelling, so that the wire will not move about (see F, Fig. 27). Now take a 4 in. × 1 in. strip of thin cardboard, roll it round a knitting needle, and glue the end down to form a narrow tube, which fits on to the wire. Glue two strong cardboard washers round the centre holes in the windmill, and thread the wire through them. Place another free washer on the wire, and then bend the end of the latter round to prevent the windmill from slipping off.

Lanterns

These may be made in different sizes to suit large or small kites. They are suspended in the same manner as wind funnels and tassels. Fig. 28 illustrates the stages in making them.

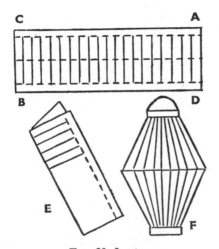

FIG. 28. Lantern

A square of thin cardboard will make two lanterns. Cut it in half. Take one of the halves and mark a narrow margin at the top and the bottom. Crease the margin lines with a blunt knife. Fold the piece in half lengthways. Make a crease at the fold. Cut slits up to the margins, as at E, and open out again.

Glue reinforcing strips along the margins. Glue AD to CB. Attach string or thin wire in the form of a loop to make a handle. Compress the top and the bottom, so that the lantern will assume the shape shown at F.

Fringes (Fig. 29)

These are simply strips of paper, folded and cut in the manner shown. Paste the bottom margin round the kite strings. The small V-shapes in the margin indicate where to cut slits, which will help when the fringes are formed in curves.

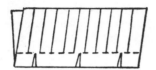

Fig. 29. Fringes

Tail Pieces (Fig. 30)

The neatest method of making these is to take pieces of paper, and fold them as indicated. It is sometimes necessary to make a tail lighter or heavier, by altering the number of paper pieces it carries. Therefore, to make this adjustment easy, the pieces are tied to the string by means of a clove hitch, as illustrated in the section on 'Knots and Hitches' in this chapter.

Fig. 30. Kite tails

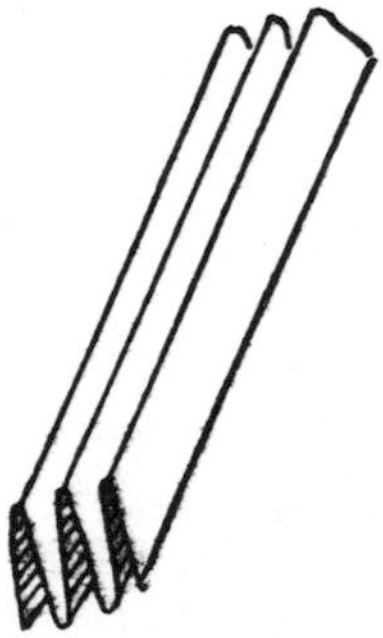

Buzzers

A strip of paper is folded in half and glued, by means of a margin, round a convenient string or frame piece. The edges of the paper vibrate in the wind.

FIG. 31. Designs

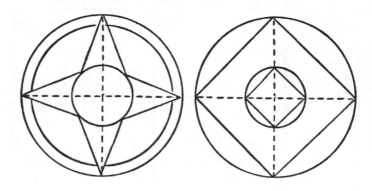

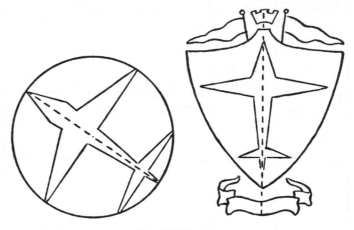

Fig. 32. Designs

Climbing Discs

Make circles, with centre holes, from thin cardboard. They may be covered with metalled paper, so that they shine in the light. Cut a slit up to the centre hole, by means of which the discs are placed on the line. Agitate the latter and the wind will carry them up to the top.

Pennants

A pennant is a long narrow flag, and one may be attached to the top of a kite backbone.

Cut a strip of tissue paper, measuring 5 in. × 20 in. Fold it in half to make a length of 10 in. Now cut it so that one end narrows to a point. Open it out, and glue a 1 in. length of $\frac{3}{16}$ in. diameter dowelling along the centre. Paste the edges, and bring the two parts together.

Another style may be made in the same way, but instead of its tapering to a point, cut the end in a V-shape. The pennants may be left plain, or decorated with simple designs. Where a kite club is formed, the pennants may bear the club emblem.

Designs

The appearance of a kite is improved by the use of effective design, which should be simple and bold and finished in deep colours. Two examples are offered in Fig. 31. These may be enlarged to a suitable size for a particular kite by increasing the size of the squares and then copying the patterns on them. This work is done not directly on to the kite cover, but on a separate sheet of paper. The pattern is then transferred to the cover either by means of carbon paper; or the pattern is coloured, cut out and then glued on to the cover. Figs. 32 and 33 show some simple but effective designs.

Kite Anchor

Here is a very useful device to which the line may be temporarily attached while the kite is in flight. This enables both hands to be free for a while, which on occasions is a welcome and useful relief.

Fig. 34 shows the component parts and the assembled anchor.

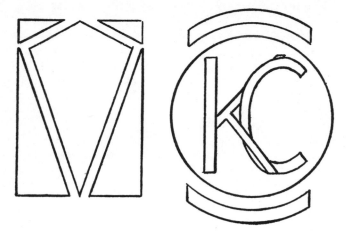

FIG. 33. Designs

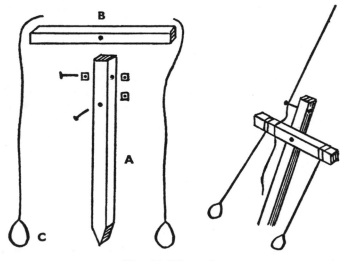

FIG. 34. Kite anchor

A is the upright bar which is 2 ft. 6 in. in length and formed from hardwood, 1½ in. square. Shape it to a point at one end, as shown. Drill two holes, ¼ in. diameter; one through the side at a point which is 2 in. from the top; the other, through the front, 6 in. from the top.

The crossbar, B, is formed from hardwood which is 1 in. square and 1 ft. 6 in. in length. Drill a hole, ¼ in. diameter, through the centre. Take two pieces of strong cord about 5 ft. in length, and make one end of each into a loop, as at C. These act as stirrups.

Now fit a 5 in. × ¼ in. diameter bolt with the thread running up to the head, into the side hole of the upright bar A. Two nuts are used to lock the bolt in position, so that 3 in. of it projects from one side of the bar. Next, fasten the two wooden pieces together with a 3 in. × ¼ in. diameter bolt.

To use the anchor, first drive the pointed end of the bar into the ground. Slip the feet into the cord loops, and bind round and tie the other ends to the crossbar so that the cords are taut. When the kite line is wrapped round the top bolt for a few times, the kite is securely anchored for as long as the operator wishes. The anchor, because it can be dismantled quickly, may be easily carried from place to place.

Shield (Fig. 35)

The suggestion for the award of a shield in club or inter-club competitions is found in Chapter 11, under the heading No. 4, 'Arrange Activities'.

The squares in dotted lines may be enlarged to a suitable size on paper, and the design copied on them. Transfer the design, by means of carbon paper, to plywood about ⅜ in. in thickness. Cut out the shield with a fretsaw, and then paint in suitable colours. When the paint is dry, a wall hanger or a strut is fixed to the back and the shield is complete.

Protecting Covers

Kites, when not in use, may be protected by storing them in large polythene bags, or bags made from sheets of strong brown paper, provided with string handles, by which they may be suspended from a wall. It may be difficult to do this in the case of a box kite, owing to its shape, but at least it may also be suspended from a wall when not in use. This will do much to prevent accidental damage.

Anemometer

This is an instrument for measuring the speed of the wind, and a simple type is shown in Fig. 36.

The crosspieces, A and B, are formed from $\frac{1}{8}$ in. × 1 in. stripwood. Each piece is 3 ft. in length. They are joined together at right angles at the centre. Use glue and small fine nails. Check with a set square to ensure that the angles are true. Drill a small hole exactly at the centre. Now take two large glass or wooden beads about 18 mm. in diameter and place them on the crossbars, one at the top and one underneath, exactly over the centre hole in the bars. Glue the beads in position and when the glue has set, pack round the beads with plastic wood, as at C. Allow sufficient time for the plastic wood to harden. Note that the hole in the crossbars is the same diameter as the holes in the beads. Following this, fix four small cups, D, to the ends of the crossbars. Use table-tennis balls, cut in halves with a sharp knife. Screw them in position, using $\frac{1}{4}$ in. screws. The cups are fixed underneath the crossbars, and small $\frac{1}{8}$ in. thick blocks of stripwood are glued above them.

The next stage is to make the spindle, E. The base is two cotton reels, glued together, into the holes of which is inserted a piece of dowelling, which is glued in place and must be a tight fit. The dowelling is cut off level with the top and bottom of the reels. A strong knitting needle is required, of such a diameter that the crossbars revolve freely but not too loosely on it. Drill a hole in the dowelling in the reel, and drive the needle securely into it. Slip a few 18 mm. beads on to the needle with a small washer on top of them.

The third stage is to make the stand, F. This is a piece of $\frac{1}{4}$ in. plywood, 3 ft. square, and strengthened underneath with battens, which is screwed to an upright bar of convenient height. The bar may be pointed at the end, so that it can be driven into the ground; or it may be attached to a base-piece, G. Drill a hole at one corner of the stand, F, and insert a $1\frac{1}{4}$ in. length of dowelling, H, and paint it red. This is the marker. One of the cups is also painted red. Place the crossbars on the spindle, and the anemometer is ready for use.

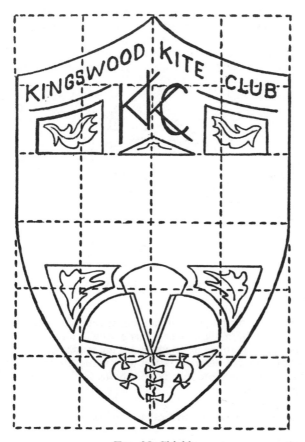

FIG. 35. Shield

If it is to be left permanently out of doors, then it may be given a coat of size, and when this is dry, enamelled in a suitable colour which offers a strong contrast to the red cup and marker.

In order to calculate the speed of the wind, one must first count the number of times which the red cup passes the red marker in

D

the space of one minute. This having been done, the speed in miles per hour can be estimated by an arithmetical calculation. It will be realized that the red cup, as it is blown by the wind, describes the circumference of a circle, the diameter of which is 3 ft. which the reader will realize is the length of the arms.

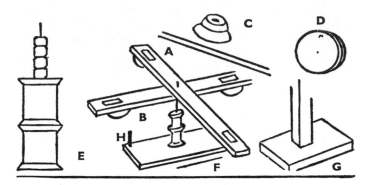

FIG. 36. Anemometer

The measurement of this circumference is found by multiplying the diameter by π ($\frac{22}{7}$). When this result is multiplied by the number of revolutions in one minute, the reader will then have found the speed of the wind in feet per minute. From this he can then calculate the speed in miles per hour.

For example:

Number of revolutions in 1 minute = 80.

Therefore speed in feet per minute $= \dfrac{3 \times 22 \times 80}{1 \times 7 \times 1}$

Therefore speed in miles per hour $= \dfrac{3 \times 22 \times 80 \times 60}{1 \times 7 \times 1 \times 5,280}$

$$= \frac{60}{7} = 8\frac{4}{7}$$

This size of anemometer is only adequate for registering wind speeds of up to 18 m.p.h. For greater accuracy, and for registering higher wind speeds, it is advisable to construct a larger instrument.

Weather Vane

A simple model is shown in Fig. 37. The spindle, A, is the same as the one used for the anemometer, but three cotton reels are used. The arm, B, is formed from ½ in. diameter dowelling, which is 1 ft. 6 in. in length. Drill a hole through the centre, of such a diameter that the arm will turn freely on the spindle. Make

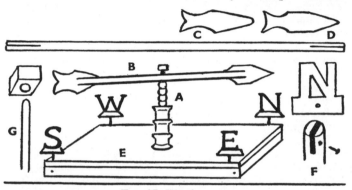

FIG. 37. Weather vane

fine saw cuts, which are 3 in. in length at each end of the arm. Next, cut the two shapes, C and D, from thin tin and make them 6 in. in length and 3 in. at the widest points. Insert these in the saw cuts, and secure them by means of glue and fine nails driven through the arm.

Now prepare the stand. For the base piece, E, use ¼ in. plywood or hardboard which is 2 ft. square and battened underneath to prevent it warping. Cut the cardinal points from thin tin or plastic. Each letter is cut from a 3 in. square of the material and is pegged to a small piece of dowelling as at F. Drill holes at the corners of the base piece and insert the pegs. Glue them securely in place. The base piece is mounted on a centre column, as for the anemometer, but in this case it is round in shape.

Assemble the vane by slipping the arm on the spindle. Place a brass washer above and below the arm. Make a cap from a small block of wood, as shown at G, and wedge this on top of the spindle by means of a centre hole, drilled half way through. Make this hole a little less in diameter than that of the spindle, so that the cap needs tapping home with a mallet. Secure with glue. The arms should balance evenly on the spindle and should revolve freely. Paint the vane in black enamel, first applying a coat of size to the wooden parts. Lubricate the hole in the arm with a little fine machine oil.

The vane may be fixed at some convenient place which is open to the wind: for example, to the top of a shed, or a post. It must be secured so that the base is truly horizontal and the spindle truly vertical.

The cardinal points are found in the first place by means of a compass, and the vane is set up to correspond to compass reading.

Compass

Though a good compass can be bought quite reasonably, some readers may find it interesting to make this simple type for themselves (Fig. 38).

The first stage is to make a compass card, A, which is 2 in. in diameter. Draw two concentric circles on thin card; the outer one is 2 in. in diameter; the inner one is 1 in. in diameter. Mark on it the cardinal points, as shown. Cut out the centre portion.

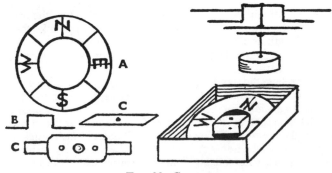

Fig. 38. Compass

Next, make the pieces B and C from thin card. B has a raised part in the centre, and from the underside of this a small depression is made by means of a round point. C is a flat strip with a small hole punched in the centre. Magnetize a steel safety razor blade by drawing a magnet across it, one way only. Before this is done, for safety's sake, place the blade in a vice and blunt the edges with a fine file. Glue the blade to the underside of the flat strip. Now, make a small cardboard box to house the compass, with sufficient clearance for the compass card to turn freely in it.

Assemble the parts upon a needle which is stuck into a piece of cork. Glue the strips B and C to the underside of the compass card; B so that the raised part fits through the centre hole; and C so that the blade is underneath. Glue two small beads above and below the hole in the strip C. The top of the needle rests in the small depression in the raised part of B.

CHAPTER EIGHT

How kites fly

WHEN a kite is flown the operator may have wondered how this is made possible. A kite is heavier than air, and yet the air supports it, just as water supports a boat. Not only that, the air lifts the kite, as it lifts the wings of an aeroplane, and so the kite climbs upwards. But it may happen that the wind tends to drive it backwards and downwards, and this is where the kite line plays its part. When it is taut the backward and downward travel is checked, and the kite is enabled to climb. This upward movement is improved, on occasions, by the operator as he runs along, holding the line and lengthening it as required. After the flight the kite is brought down to the ground again.

In the above statement four forces are mentioned or implied which need further explanation. They are the forces of resistance; upward thrust or lift; downward pull or gravity, and propulsion. It may be said that a kite flies because ways and means have been found to use these forces to the best advantage. This may be seen as each is considered in turn.

The first is called resistance. By this it is meant that air exerts a force against, that is, opposes, an object moving through it, as the following simple examples will show. Take a piece of cardboard, hold it in a horizontal position, and move it from side to side. The board cuts easily and quickly through the air, the reason being that there is very little resistance offered to the board. Now use the latter as a fan, that is in an upright position. The difference is immediately felt. There is definite opposition to the movement of the board, as if the air were acting like a brake to slow it down.

Again, this resistance is felt whenever anyone is out walking. Even on a calm day he is aware of the air brushing against him; and on a windy day the air becomes a strong opposing force, to overcome which the walker has to increase his efforts.

In these examples the moving objects are displacing the air as a boat displaces water, and the air opposes the action. It rubs against the objects, and this action is like that of a brake. Air clings to the surfaces of things, tending to slow them down and to stop them, in other words, to overcome the power which is moving them along.

There is, however, another force which is present, acting in an upward direction. This may be proved in a very simple way. Place a piece of writing paper on a table and blow along the top of the table. The paper tends to rise and move forward. In passing, this was one of the ways in which Sir George Cayley demonstrated the lifting property of air. This force, called upward thrust, is evident when a leaf or a piece of paper are being blown about in the wind, and when an aeroplane or a kite is flying.

Anyone who has ever flown a kite has used this force to prevent its falling to the ground. The operator sets out to fly his kite. He lays it on the ground, and holding the kite line, he runs forward against the wind. In this action the front or leading edge of the kite is pulled against the air, causing it to rise off the ground. It gradually climbs at a shallow angle because the air is being exerted in an upward direction. As long as the correct angle or inclination of the kite is maintained, this upward thrust will operate effectively. In addition, as a result of the wind's flowing around the sides of the kite, a partial vacuum is formed above its upper side. This also helps the kite to rise in a steady manner, and the fact that this vacuum exists explains why the kite is said to sail on the air.

It will be seen in what has just been said that in order to fly a kite it must present an inclined surface to the wind. In other words, the kite must meet the wind at an angle as it moves forward. This angle is called the angle of incidence. The more the kite is inclined towards the horizontal, up to a certain fixed point, the better it will climb. As the kite moves nearer to the vertical position, it offers a larger target for air resistance, which will drive it backwards because the upward thrust cannot operate effectively. On the other hand, as the kite moves nearer to the horizontal position (up to a certain fixed point) part of the air resistance is converted into a force acting in an upward direction. Of course, if the kite approaches too much towards the horizontal position, then again the upward thrust is progressively weakened, and the kite will not climb.

These points may be proved quite easily. Fly a kite from a fixed position in a gentle breeze. Left to its own devices it will tend towards the vertical position. Because of this position or angle the kite will be sluggish in rising, and at the same time will be driven backwards. It may eventually assume the vertical position, and consequently make one of those annoying dives to earth. In this event, the upward thrust has been made of no effect and the kite responds to a downward pull.

Again, fly a kite in a strong wind. The kite will be eager to climb and to attain an overhead position. This is due to the fact that the greater wind pressure and the stronger pull on the line have caused the kite to assume an angle at which it responds readily to the upward thrust.

But if for some reason the kite is prevented from maintaining the correct angle, and it moves too far in the direction of the horizontal position, then it becomes unsteady in flight and unless the position can be rectified, the kite will respond to the downward pull, and this is the next force to be considered.

Downward pull is due to the weight of the kite, and weight is an important factor. A kite is heavier than air, and ways have to be found to overcome this disadvantage. Obviously, one thing to do is to make the kite as light as possible. A kite which is not made according to this rule is overloaded, and the effect of this will be the same as when an aeroplane is overloaded. Nevertheless, even when a kite is as light as possible in relation to its size it is still subject to the influence of downward pull.

This pull is called the force of gravity. Everything falls to the ground if it is not held up by some means. It is the earth which attracts things. If there were no such attraction, then everything would be shot off into space by the force of the earth's rotation. Gravity then is force exerted by the earth, to which all bodies are subject; a force manifested in a downward pull.

At this point reference may be made to what is called the centre of gravity. This may be defined as the point where the downward pull is concentrated; or again, as that point in a body about which the whole weight is evenly balanced. The centre of gravity may be found by the rules of geometry; or by experiment. As an example of the latter, a rod may be suspended by a string which is looped over a nail. If a weighted length of string is tied to the nail it will indicate the point where the centre of gravity is situated. This point comes where the string crosses the rod. It is here that the downward pull is concentrated; it is here that the whole weight is evenly balanced.

But as far as kite flying is concerned, this is not the whole story. The centre of gravity is not only the point where downward pull is concentrated; it is also the point where the lines of the other forces should meet or intersect—these forces being upward thrust, resistance and propulsion. If this is to be achieved, then the kite must be properly balanced. Should there be any mistake in this respect, then the kite will be unsteady in flight. To correct this instability and to bring the forces into line, the operator may have to make a good many adjustments, such as lengthening or shortening the tail or moving the kite line. Successful kite flying is very much the outcome of such practices.

It has been explained, so far, that a kite in flight is subject to the influence of the forces of resistance, upward thrust and downward pull. To these a fourth must be added, which as yet has only been briefly mentioned, and this is propulsion. It might be wondered at first why this should be attributed to a kite, since it has no motor. A moment's reflection, however, will make it plain to the reader that propulsion is supplied by the operator and the kite line. The line, as it were, acts as a motor to the kite, or to put it in another way, transmits the power supplied by the operator to the kite.

Propulsion is effective according to the use which is made of the kite line. For example, suppose a kite is being flown in a light breeze. If the line is slack, the kite will tend to move backwards and downwards. To correct this the operator tightens the line and maybe runs forward. It is just as if a motor had been switched on. The kite tends to move forwards and upwards, in response to the power exerted by the line. This power causes the kite to assume an effective angle whereby resistance is converted into upward thrust.

This general statement, however, must be qualified by the following facts. The more line there is released, the more resistance there is created. Again, the longer the line, the greater the weight the kite has to support. As a result, the kite may sag off downwind. This movement backwards tends to affect the angle of incidence, so that upward thrust decreases. Thus it will be seen that the propulsion supplied by the line is influenced by the amount which is released.

It may be helpful at this point to provide a brief summary of the chapter so far. A kite in flight is subject to the influence of four forces, namely: resistance; upward thrust; downward pull; and propulsion. Resistance is the opposition exerted by the air to an object moving through it. Upward thrust is the part of this resistance which is converted into a lifting force. Downward pull is due to the weight of the kite, which, because of its weight, is attracted to the earth. Downward pull is said to be concentrated at that point in a body which is called the centre of gravity. Propulsion is the force exerted by the kite line, which acts as a motor to the kite. These forces act in opposition in the horizontal and the vertical direction: resistance and propulsion in the horizontal, and downward pull and upward thrust in the vertical. In order for these forces to act in such a way that makes flight possible, they must pass in continuous lines through the centre of gravity. If they do not, then the kite is unstable in flight, because the forces are being exerted at different points. The forces must be expended in opposite directions and along continuous lines.

In order to meet with this requirement the kite must present a correctly inclined surface to the wind. It must also be properly balanced. And because balance is so important it becomes the subject of further study.

As has been said, balance is obtained by an even distribution of weight around the centre of gravity, or mass centre, as it is also termed. As far as the practical application of this principle is concerned, the writer has found it helpful to adopt the following procedure. Take a kite with a main central strut or backbone. There is a point on this backbone where the kite will balance on the end of a rod. When the point has been located it may be marked with a pencil. It is the centre of gravity or mass centre.

So far it has been established that at this centre the kite balances on the end of a rod, because there is an even distribution of weight around the centre. The force of gravity is pulling equally on all sides. The kite is showing what is called longitudinal and lateral balance. The next thing to do is to find ways and means of keeping this two-way balance when the kite is in flight.

The first thing to do in this search for balance is to think of a kite in flight. The air, in meeting it and flowing around it, creates disturbances which tend to make the kite unsteady. For example, it may be liable to dip backwards and forwards. The kite does not show longitudinal balance. In order to improve this balance, the kite line must be tied in the right position. A kite with the line fixed at the right point, generally slightly ahead of the centre of gravity, shows longitudinal stability, in other words, it keeps on an even keel.

There is another fault which will upset a kite in flight. Owing to the disturbances it encounters, it may tend to sway from side to side. It lacks lateral balance. The latter is improved by the use of effective dihedral. In an aeroplane, dihedral is the angle between the horizontal surface of a wing and the fuselage. As seen from the front, the wings form a shallow V-shape. In a kite, dihedral is secured by the bowing of the crossbar or bars. In effect this means, that if the kite tips to one side, then the edge of that side which is forced down presses against the air underneath it. At the same time the edge of the other side which is forced up presses against the air above it. This increases the pressure of air in both places, with the result that one side is lifted up and the other side is pushed down and so balance is restored. Again, lateral balance is improved in those cases where the bridle is fixed crossways on the kite.

The longitudinal and the lateral balance of a kite is illustrated in the action of a pair of scales. If an equal weight is placed on the scale pans, and one side is tipped down, the arm will return to a position of equipoise. The scales demonstrate stable equilibrium, which means the tendency of a body to return to a position of rest when moved or disturbed.

There is another item which should be mentioned, and it is directional steadiness. Without this a kite may tend to move erratically from its course. Such deviation is called yawing. Directional stability is improved by the use of a flexible tail, which acts like the rudder of a boat.

The degree of perfection which is implied in the above requirements is not achieved by written instructions alone. They are but the signposts pointing the way to a desirable goal. When all has been said which may profitably be said, it still remains for the kite flyer to strive towards the goal by constant practice. By a process of trial and error, eliminating faults one by one, sure progress is made towards the goal of successful kite flying. The latter will now be further considered under a separate heading.

FLYING A KITE

In dealing with this subject, for the sake of clarity, some things which have already been dealt with will be mentioned again, and, if necessary, will receive further comment.

First to be considered is the place from which the kite is flown. There are certain do's and don't's which operate here. For example, avoid a spot where the kite might become entangled with trees or overhead wires, or where it might sail over a busy road. A good site is one where there is room to move about freely without causing annoyance to others. This applies particularly when several kites are being flown. It is exasperating if the lines get mixed up. Kite flyers, like anglers, give one another sufficient room in which to enjoy their pastime.

Next, a word about weather conditions. It is the aim and intent of the enthusiast to fly his kite successfully under varying conditions. He regards them as a challenge to his skill. At the same time he is not so misguided as to see a challenge in a gale. He knows that because a kite is, after all, but a frail craft, there are limits to its capabilities. In this respect, common sense is a good guide.

The following are instances of different flying conditions. On a warm calm day the air seems to be still. But this is only comparatively so. Although there is little movement in a horizontal direction, there is upward activity. This is due to rising currents of air, called thermic currents. They will be found, for example, above ploughed fields, moorland and where buildings are grouped together. The familiar heat shimmer is an indication of this rising air. On the other hand, on such a day, there will be colder descending air where there is water, marsh or meadow.

Then there comes a day when the wind is blowing. There can be variation in its movement. For example, it may be a fitful wind. Again, and to the point here, it may meet an obstacle such as a hill, a cliff, or a building, in which case it is deflected upwards. The strength of the up-current will depend upon the force of the wind, and the size of the obstacle it meets.

Rising currents are a means whereby birds can soar, that is, fly without flapping their wings. Again, the glider pilot derives benefit from them. It follows, therefore, that, on occasions, they may prove to be helpful to the kite flyer.

(Please note. Further information on weather conditions is given in Chapter 10.)

We turn now from the weather to the kite. Before flying it, its size must be taken into account. Sometimes the enthusiast is tempted to build an outsize one. Though it may be the object of interest and admiration, the owner might not have realized that in flying large kites both skill and strength are needed. Someone has said that a 6-ft. kite pulls like a cart-horse. It follows then that one half this size, in a fairly strong wind and when a considerable amount of line has been released, can exert a strong pull. For this reason, the size in this book is limited to 3 ft. 6 in. This is a convenient and manageable size range for the beginner. Later on, if desired, the reader may make larger sizes by increasing the measurements given.

The next thing to do is to inspect the kite. First, check the bridle and the line, to see that they are secure and that the line runs freely on the reel. Secondly, test the bracing and bowstrings to make sure that they are taut. The method of tying these, which is shown in Chapter 7, under the heading 'Knots and Hitches', will ensure that they can be tightened, if necessary. Thirdly, inspect the cover to ascertain whether it is secure and in good condition. This is very important in the case of a paper cover, as it can easily get damaged.

The method of flying the kite is as follows. A length of line is released. A friend holds the kite, or if no help is at hand, it is laid on the ground. The operator then runs forward against the wind. The length of the run and the speed required depend upon the force of the wind. The kite will gradually rise at a shallow angle. The operator, still moving, releases more line, the kite meanwhile responding to upward thrust. From then on it is largely a matter of movement on the part of the operator when called for, and of manipulating the line. Even on a fairly calm day the action of running causes a wind that will lift the kite, and this is aided by a gradual release of the line, and by choosing a place where there may be rising currents of air.

The height which a kite may reach is dependent very largely upon the amount of line which is released. If conditions be favourable, it will climb steadily until the weight of the line begins to be felt. It will rise all the time that the upward thrust is strong enough to overcome the downward pull, due to the weight of the kite and the line. The speed of the ascent is increased by a series of steady pulls on the line. In bringing the kite down, allow it to describe a descending curve, meanwhile move towards it, and carefully wind in the line. The kite should not be pulled down by brute force. Care is particularly needed for the last few feet of descent. The kite will behave wildly if the line is wound in too fast.

Success in kite flying comes, as it comes in other activities, by acquiring skill through practice. Theory may be good, but, for example, it is only when the pilot or the driver takes over that he gets the necessary 'feel' of his machine; it is only by handling his machine that he discovers what he and it can do in a given situation. So it is with kite flying. And let it be said that it is in this very fact that much of the interest of kite flying is found. If a kite were as mechanical in its movements as a clockwork train on a circular track, then the interest would be lost. It is the spontaneous response of a kite to variable weather conditions which sustains interest. The operator is in control, and finds much pleasure in this fact. There is a certain analogy between kite flying and both gliding and sailing. One person, as it were, becomes part of a craft which is very responsive to the elements and to his controlling hand.

As far as kite styles are concerned, it may be said that today they mainly belong to two classes: the box and the flat type. The box kite flies after the manner of an aeroplane, that is, at a small angle to the wind. Its shape helps to keep it from side-slipping, which means a sideways and downwards movement. The shape improves stability. The box kite has a good lift, that is to say, it climbs well, and can be readily brought to a nearly overhead position. The flat-type kite flies at a larger angle to the wind, and in many cases balance is obtained by the use of a flexible tail. It has a lively manner and is more suited than the box to aerial acrobatics. By skilful use of the line it will dive and dart about in the air in a most interesting way.

It will therefore be seen that the choice of a kite depends upon what one wishes to do with it. If the aim is to fly high, then the box type is the choice. If on the other hand, the idea is to carry out aerial manœuvres, then the flat or plane kite, as it is also called, is the one to use.

Note 1. A Useful Hint.

For steadying a kite in flight, when other methods fail, tie a piece of thin material about the size of a man's handkerchief,

to the end of the tail string. The author has found this to be very
effective.

Note 2.   Important.

Readers are advised to make inquiries at their local police
station as to whether there are any bye-laws or local regulations,
governing kite flying, particularly regarding the height to which
they may be flown.

PART TWO

Getting the Most from Your Hobby

CHAPTER NINE

Make your own style of kite

THE reader will find in this and the following chapters a variety of things which he can do, to enable him to get the utmost satisfaction from kites and kite flying. These things to do, divided into sections, are as follows:

> *Make your own style of kite.*
> *Be weather-wise.*
> *Form a club.*
> *Arrange activities.*

It is hoped that the time spent in studying them will be amply repaid.

Although many different kites are described in this book, this suggestion may appeal to the reader who is keen on experimental work. Kites can be made in many shapes, and as long as the rules of balance, lightness and strength are kept in mind, they should fly well. On this point J. G. Wood once wrote: 'The old theory used to be that a very slight deviation from accurate proportions in a kite must certainly prove fatal to its powers of flight; but of late years . . . we have discovered that so long as certain rules of symmetry are observed, that is, so long as one side fairly balances the other, there is almost no conceivable shape that may not be made to mount up as a kite into the sky.' Obviously then there is great opportunity for individual design; and this being so, it may be helpful to the would-be designer to have some guidance in how to begin and how to carry the project through. The following step-by-step instructions serve this purpose.

Finding a Design

The first thing to do is to think of a suitable design. This is not difficult. The silhouette of a bird or a plane may suggest a shape. Again, variations of the box-kite theme may be worked out. There are also certain basic forms, with which one might experiment—the square, the oblong, the triangle, the diamond and the circle. The designer works on the shape or shapes which appeal to him. He arranges, combines or alters them, and so evolves a satisfactory plan on the drawing board. As an example of this, we select three shapes and combine them in a pleasing design (see Fig. 39).

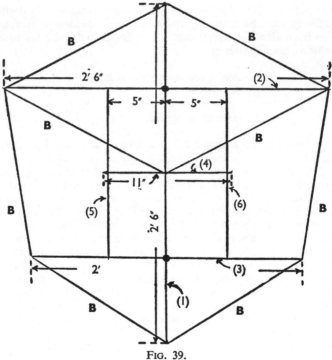

FIG. 39.

Drawing the Design

The next step is to decide the overall size of the kite, so that the design can be worked out to scale on paper. The reader is invited at this point to produce his own scale plan from the full-size measurements given. The kite shown is 2 ft. 6 in. in length, and 2 ft. 6 in. at its widest part. These measurements are scaled down to one-sixth, and everything is drawn to this proportion.

The procedure is as follows. Draw the backbone first at the centre of the paper. This is the key piece upon which everything else depends. Now add the lines representing the two crossbars, which support the wing and the tail. The position of crossbars in kite design depends upon the general shape and proportions. The largest part of this kite is the diamond-shaped wing, which is 2 ft. 6 in. in width and half the length of the backbone. The top crossbar is drawn across the centre of the wing.

The next item is the triangular tail. In the interests of a pleasing design it is made smaller than the wing, being 2 ft. in width and occupying one quarter of the length of the backbone. Draw a line representing the tail crossbar.

In the diagram two vertical struts will be seen, connected to the crossbars. They form the body supports, and on the actual kite are fixed 5 in. from each side of the backbone. Add a small crossbar at the centre of the backbone, and the framework is complete. Note that on the plan being made, full-size measurements relating to every part are given. To complete the plan, draw lines representing the bracing strings. Two large dots indicate the bridle tying points at the backbone junctions.

Construction

The kite can now be built with the plan for a guide. The following are the materials recommended. Stripwood, $\frac{3}{8}$ in. square for the backbone, and $\frac{1}{4}$ in. square for the struts; split cane for the crossbars; paper or cloth for the cover. To these are added binding thread, bracing string, bridle string and kite line.

Cut the backbone, and groove it at the top and bottom. Prepare the crossbars in the same way, and then bow them by the method described in Chapters 1–6. The large one is curved to a depth of $2\frac{1}{4}$ in.; the smaller one 2 in., and the 11 in. centre crossbar about $\frac{1}{2}$ in. Secure these to the backbone. Glue small blocks on either side to keep them parallel. Attach the vertical struts. Now brace the framework and test it for firmness.

Next add the cover which may be lightweight cloth or unbleached greaseproof paper. Attach the bridle to the backbone in the form of a loop, and to this, tie the kite line. The bridle is twice the length of the kite. A tail, 6 ft. in length, is tied to the bottom of the backbone.

Testing

The kite is now ready to be tested in different flying conditions. Make any necessary adjustments to suit the occasion. Calculate the speed of the wind by the help of the Beaufort Wind Scale (see p. 128). When you have done this, note whether at a given speed the tail is just right, or has to be weighted or lightened. Take note also whether the position of the kite line has to be altered. Such on-the-spot observations and adjustments are vital in attaining the skill so necessary for successful kite flying.

The reader may also be interested in the style of the Hargrave box kite, seen in Plate IV. On the basis of the illustration a scale plan could be prepared for guidance in the construction of the kite. As will be seen, it consists of a double framework, linked together by two main centre longerons. On the other hand, the bands could be linked together by means of four corner longerons.

CHAPTER TEN

Be weather-wise

THE next suggestion for getting the most from kites is to focus one's attention on an important subject—the weather. The close connexion between kite flying and the weather is apparent to the most casual observer. There are days when conditions are ideal; there are days when they are fairly good; there are days when they are bad. And there are times when the weather varies from hour to hour. A day which seems to be promising at the start does not keep its promise; and one which might not look too good at first turns out to be better than was expected. Because of this changeable weather it is really necessary to have some understanding first, of the kite itself—particularly of making adjustments in different flying conditions; and second, of the weather, which is the immediate subject. And let it be said that to understand the weather does not imply that one must be an expert in meteorology. All that is contemplated is a working knowledge that will help the kite flyer to get the most from his hobby. The aim in this section is to point out some of the ways and means whereby this knowledge may be gained. One way is to study the clouds.

Clouds

The reader may often have noticed their changing pattern as they move along. This panorama is one of the wonders of nature—a fascinating scene wherein every cloud is subject to change, and no two are identical, and some combine in form. Yet, although there is this state of flux, clouds are classified and names given to them. True, it is not always easy for the amateur to place them in the groups to which they belong. But in due course, by sustained observation, he may be able to do this. A guide in such study will be found in the list of the ten main types of cloud, printed below, as given in the International Cloud Atlas.

Classification

1. CIRRUS, 'detached clouds of delicate appearance, fibrous structure, without true shadows, usually white in colour'.

2. CIRRO-CUMULUS, 'small rounded masses or white flakes without shadows, arranged in groups or lines, or sometimes in the form of ripples such as those formed on the seashore'.
3. CIRRO-STRATUS, 'thin veil of whitish cloud, sometimes entirely diffuse and giving the sky a milky appearance, sometimes showing a fibrous structure'.
4. ALTO-CUMULUS, 'rounded masses or discs, more or less large, arranged in groups, in lines or in rows, following one or two directions and sometimes so crowded together that their edges are joined'.
5. ALTO-STRATUS, 'a veil of a colour more or less grey'.
6. STRATO-CUMULUS, 'large, lumpy masses or rolls of dull, grey cloud frequently covering the whole sky and sometimes giving it an undulating appearance'.
7. STRATUS, 'a uniform layer of cloud, like fog in appearance but not lying on the ground'.
8. NIMBO-STRATUS, 'a low layer of structureless and rainy-looking cloud, sombre grey in colour'.
9. CUMULUS, 'thick cloud whose summit is dome-shaped and exhibits protuberances, while the base is nearly horizontal'.
10. CUMULO-NIMBUS, 'great masses of cloud rising in the form of mountainous towers of which the upper parts, of fibrous texture, sometimes spread out in the form of an anvil'.

Clouds occur at different heights, and this fact is indicated by the use of the prefixes, cirro and alto. Cirro denotes those which are between 25,000 and 35,000 feet up; and alto those between 10,000 and 25,000 feet up. The lower layer occurs mainly between 500 and 7,000 feet up (Nos. 6–10}

Clouds and Weather

Generally speaking, the higher the clouds, the better the weather is likely to be; the lower the clouds, the worse it is likely to be. In particular, three factors to be taken into account are: movement, change and colour. The following are examples of these. Small cirrus clouds—'mare's tails'—when they thicken and become lower, are a sign that rain is on the way. Cirro-cumulus—'mackerel sky'—heralds the approach of rain, and on occasions, of thunder. Cumulus clouds, when they expand early in the day, are also a warning that rain will fall later. Cumulonimbus becomes 'the thunder-cloud' when its top at the front becomes extended so that the whole cloud looks like an anvil. This may be accompanied by a sudden cool breeze, which travels in an opposite direction to that of the actual wind at the time. The cloud and the breeze are signs that a storm is about to break.

Clouds, however, are not only associated with rain and storm. They may also indicate fine weather. As an example there is the cirrus, previously mentioned, which now appears in a more promising role. If it does not thicken and seems to be at a standstill or only moving slowly, in a region of high pressure, then it means fine weather. The 'fair weather cumulus' is another example. It does not grow bigger, has no marked upward bulges and moves slowly along. These are the clouds which are often to be seen on a warm summer day.

In the list and the examples given, colour is associated with changes in the weather. It ranges from the white of cirro-cumulus to the dark grey of nimbo-stratus. The association is shown in further instances of sky colours, the first of which occurs in the old saying:

> *Red sky at night, shepherd's delight*
> *Red sky in the morning, shepherd's warning.*

It has been estimated that this is true about three times out of five. The second illustration adds another colour to the range: yellow. A watery yellow sunset is a sign of coming rain; a bright yellow sunset is a token of an approaching high wind. Again, a golden ring round the moon is a warning that a storm is on the way. In the last place, there is the rainbow. This multi-coloured arc appears opposite to the sun, and is formed by refraction and reflection of its light through falling raindrops. If the sun is in the east, and the rainbow is in the west and a west wind is blowing, then rain is moving towards the observer. If the sun is in the west and the rainbow is in the east and a west wind is blowing, then rain is moving away from the observer.

Clouds then are an index of weather changes; and so is the wind, which we now consider.

Wind

The subject is of immediate interest to the kite flyer, for the wind is in turn both his friend and his foe. He cannot alter this fact, but he may gain some knowledge of these different moods which may stand him in good stead. Under this heading brief comment will be made upon each of the following items: first, wind and weather; second, estimating wind direction; and third, estimating wind speed.

Wind and Weather

As far as the British area is concerned, a general statement may be made: south-westerly winds are wet winds; north-easterly winds are dry winds. The south-westerly winds which have travelled hundreds of miles across the Atlantic have taken up a great amount of moisture on the way. When they encounter the main highlands of the area, they are forced to rise and in so doing the greater part of the moisture is squeezed out as rain. On the other hand, north-easterly winds when they prevail for a time, are usually a sign of an anticyclone over the North Sea, or even farther north-east, and anticyclones are associated with spells of fine weather.

(Additional notes on depressions and anticyclones are given at the end of this chapter.)

Estimating Wind Direction

A simple method is to wet a finger and hold it up; the side which feels cold first is the windward side. Another way is to observe the direction in which low cloud or smoke are moving. If these are not present, as an alternative, a handkerchief may be held up to flutter in the wind. By these means the operator can judge the kite's line of flight, and so will be able to guard against any possible obstructions, such as trees or overhead wires.

Estimating wind direction is also useful in making forecasts and flight records, which are described below. In these cases a weather-cock and a pocket compass are the best guides. If there is no local weather-cock, the reader might be interested in the making of a simple type, as shown in Chapter 7. On-the-spot wind checks are carried out with a compass, and it is used in conjunction with the tests mentioned in the first paragraph. When the compass is held horizontally in the hand the needle points to the magnetic north, which is not the exact geographical north. The slight variation must be ascertained in any given place in order to find the true north. For example, in England the compass points about 8 degrees west of geographical north.

Estimating Wind Speed

The Amended Beaufort Wind Scale, printed at the end of the chapter, is valuable for this purpose; as also is an anemometer. The Wind Scale was formulated in 1805 by Admiral Sir Francis Beaufort for measuring the velocity of the wind and since then has been periodically revised. An anemometer is an instrument for registering the speed of wind. Instructions for making and using a simple type are given in Chapter 7.

Estimates of wind speed are important for two reasons. In the first place, speed and strain are closely connected. For example, if wind speed is 5 m.p.h. and it increases to 10 m.p.h. then its strength intensifies and the strain on the kite increases. The strain becomes more pronounced as the kite climbs higher. Consequently, there is a stronger pull on the kite line. The larger the kite the more do these considerations have to be borne in mind. In the second place, wind speed is a factor to be noted when making weather forecasts and flight records, which are now suggested.

Weather Forecasts

It is recommended that one's own forecasts be made on the basis first, of official forecasts which are given on the radio and television and in the daily press. These general forecasts may be compared with regional forecasts, where they are given. The amateur forecaster should also take into account certain factors in his own area. These might have a bearing upon local weather conditions. For example, where there are hills and woods they act as a shield against the wind for those who are sheltered by them. A valley may cause the wind to change its course to some degree and perhaps increase its force. Again, a warm moist wind may move over flat country accompanied by only light showers. But when the wind crosses hilly country considerable rain may develop. The amateur weather man studies the area in which he lives, notes its physical features from the point of view that they may have some connexion with the local weather.

Official forecasts and reports in the press are often given together with weather maps. In order to understand the maps the following things should be noted. The positions of weather stations are indicated by small circles, and barometric pressures by numbers. Places which show the same pressure are linked by lines, called isobars. These run near to or might even pass through the stations. Wind direction is indicated by arrows. To these arrows lines may be added representing wind speed. (Refer to the Beaufort Scale for map symbols.) Again, wind speed may be indicated by numbers. Note that for a depression the arrows are turned slightly towards the centre of pressure, and they point in an anti-clockwise direction. For an anticyclone the arrows point outwards from the centre of pressure, in a clockwise direction. When one is looking at a weather map the relative positions of the isobars should be noted. If they are drawn close to one another then wind speed is greater than when they are farther apart. One other thing may be mentioned, namely that among other map symbols which are used are those which represent a warm, a cold, or an occluded front.

On the basis of such official forecasts, plus one's own observations, an attempt may be made to estimate what flying conditions will be like one, two, or more days ahead. As far as local observations are concerned, it is a good plan to make them at fixed times during the day, for example, say 8.30 a.m. and 5.30 p.m. This would provide a regular system for weather study, whereby the following items could be recorded: wind direction and speed; cloud formation; temperature and barometer readings. On the latter point, it will be remembered that a falling barometer is a sign of rainy weather, and a rising barometer, of fine weather.

Flight Records

Much pleasure is to be derived from making these and from keeping them for reference. The idea is to set down in a note-book certain comments relating to flights as they are made. The records will be mentioned again in connexion with kite clubs and competitions. In the meantime, the following gives an idea of the kind of thing in mind.

Flight Record

Date of Flight.
Base (i.e. place where kite is flown).
Cloud Formation (see list of cloud types).

Wind $\left\{\begin{array}{l}\text{Direction.} \\ \text{Speed (see Beaufort Scale).}\end{array}\right.$

Flight $\left\{\begin{array}{l}\text{Start.} \\ \text{Finish.}\end{array}\right.$

Height Attained.

Kite (Type) (i.e. box, pegtop, etc.).

Additional Comment (e.g. on behaviour of kite, adjustments to line or tail, etc.).

Base Maps

These have not been previously mentioned, and the suggestion is now offered for consideration. It is assumed that the reader does not invariably fly his kites in one place. There might be half a dozen or more favourable sites in his locality, which could be indicated on a map, covering a radius, say, of five miles. An Ordnance Survey Map would be useful in this project. It may be that one could be studied at the local library. There is a series of these maps on a scale of six inches to the mile, which contain a great amount of information. The best-known series are on a scale of one inch to the mile. With the help of one of the above, a map could be drawn on a large sheet of paper, marking for example, prominent buildings, roads, fields, hills, woods and water in different colours. As bases were found and tried they could be marked on the map, and notes on them added at the bottom of the paper. Or they might be classified according to merit as one star (1*), two star (2*), and so on. Such a means of reference would be invaluable if a club were formed and competitions were held. The latter are the subjects of the next chapter.

Depressions and Anticyclones

These notes offer additional information about the British weather, and may be found helpful in the following of official forecasts, and in estimating flying conditions beforehand.

Depressions are storms bringing wet weather. In form they are roughly oval, and sometimes measure nearly 1,000 miles from end to end and perhaps 200–300 miles across. They begin in the neighbourhood of Newfoundland, and move from west to east across the Atlantic, travelling along regular paths, according to the seasons. In summer the path lies farther north than it does in winter. The speed of travel varies. It may be sometimes about

700 miles per day. At other times one may be at a standstill for a few days. As to duration, generally speaking a depression originates and fades out within the space of one week. On an average 50 depressions move across the British Isles in a year. They occur more often in winter than in summer.

A depression is also defined as being a system with low pressure at its centre, from which pressure increases in all directions. The air at the centre is warmer than the air surrounding it, because warm air is not so dense or heavy as cold air, and consequently it exerts less pressure. The wind blows spirally towards the centre in an anti-clockwise direction in the northern hemisphere.

Certain signs herald the approach of a depression: a falling barometer, a southerly wind, a cloudy sky, and at night perhaps a halo round the moon. As the centre of the depression moves nearer, the wind may drop, the clouds become lower and threatening, and rain falls—light and scattered at first, but developing to heavy and continuous. When the storm centre has passed, the barometer gradually rises, the wind may change to north-westerly, low stratiform cloud and drizzle give way to clearing skies and sunshine. The depression gradually fades out over north-west Europe.

This description applies to a depression only in a general way, because actually no two are identical. There are variations of the general pattern, and therefore the unexpected can happen. Again, a given area may not be in the direct path of the storm centre, but to the north or south of it. In these cases there could be variation of rainfall and of wind direction.

In contrast to a depression, an anticyclone is associated with fine weather, warm to hot in summer and clear and frosty in winter. These periods of fine weather might last for days or even weeks. However, as will be seen in a moment, this is not all which may be said about anticyclonic conditions.

An anticyclone is a system in which the centre of high pressure is encircled by low pressure. The winds blow outwards from the centre in a clockwise direction. They are usually gentle winds. Anticyclonic weather varies according to the position of the centre of pressure. If it is over the British Isles in summer, then there will be summery weather: clear skies, light winds and warm to hot days. In winter it might lead to dull or foggy conditions.

If the centre lies farther north, off the western coasts, mixed weather would be the result, with bright intervals, scattered showers, winds north to north-west and perhaps temperatures below average for the time of the year. If the centre is to the south of the British Isles, then the weather is likely to be mild and humid, with cloudy skies.

There are periods when neither depressions nor anticyclones prevail. This is called unstable weather, with local developments of threatening skies, rain and perhaps thunder. In winter, unstable weather might result in cold north winds, sleet and snow.

In weather reports, among other terms which are used, there are fronts and troughs. At a warm front associated with a depression the warmer air is forced upwards and over the under-lying cold air. As the warm air rises, it cools and some of its water vapour forms into clouds producing a wide belt of rain which moves ahead of the front. In the case of a cold front, the heavier cold air meets and pushes under the warmer light air. This action leads to the formation of towering clouds, showers of rain and sometimes thunderstorms, which arrive not ahead of but at the same time as the front.

There are times when by the action of the heavier cold air the lighter warm air is lifted completely off the ground. The front is then called occluded, and since there is no warm air at ground level, there will be no rise in temperature as it passes. Many of the depressions moving over the British Isles are partially or com-pletely occluded.

Sometimes one will see on a weather map that, instead of being drawn in a rounded pattern, the isobars (lines of barometric pressure) are joined at sharper angles. These represent a trough, which is a V-shaped depression. Troughs may have warm, cold or occluded fronts. A warm front brings cloudy warm wet weather; cold or occluded fronts, heavy rain followed by better weather.

The Amended Beaufort Scale

Scale No.	Wind m.p.h.	Forecast description	Map symbol	Effects observable
0	Less than 1	Calm	⊚	Smoke rises vertically.
1	2	Light air	\	Smoke drifts. Vanes do not move.
2	5	Light breeze	\	Wind felt on face. Leaves rustle. Vanes move.
3	10	Gentle breeze	\ \	Leaves and twigs in motion. Light flags extended.
4	15	Moderate breeze	\ \	Wind raises dust and loose papers. Small branches move. Flags flap.
5	21	Fresh breeze	\ \ \	Small trees in leaf sway slightly. Wavelets on ponds and lakes.
6	28	Strong breeze	\ \ \	Large branches begin to move. Telephone wires whistle.
7	35	Moderate gale	\ \ \ \	Whole trees in motion.
8	42	Fresh gale	\ \ \ \	Twigs break off. Progress of pedestrians impeded.
9	50	Strong gale	\ \ \ \ \	Slight structural damage. Chimney pots and slates may be removed.
10	59	Whole gale	\ \ \ \ \	Trees uprooted. Much damage to buildings.
11	69	Storm	\ \ \ \ \ \	Widespread damage.
12	Over 75	Hurricane	\ \ \ \ \ \	Devastation.

CHAPTER ELEVEN

Form a Club

WHY not form a club? Something shared brings greater pleasure to all concerned. It is hoped that this section may serve to show the way in which to start a club, and also indicate its aims and activities.

First and obviously, a club must have members. This means talking the matter over with others who may be interested in the project. In some places, a suggestion to form a kite club would come as a new idea, and this could be an advantage. When two or three have been found who are willing to make a start, then a meeting could be arranged. The one who called the meeting (the convener) would act temporarily as the chairman. He should prepare beforehand an agenda, along the lines suggested.

Agenda
1. Put forward a resolution that a club be formed. If this were agreed, then appointments could be made.
2. Appointment of Officers.

   (*a*) Club Leader. As well as conducting meetings, the leader would be in charge of the running of the club.
   (*b*) Secretary. On appointment, the secretary would proceed to take notes of the meeting taking place. As well as recording and reading the minutes of meetings, he would attend to correspondence and the like.
   (*c*) Treasurer. He would be responsible for club funds.
   (Additional Note. In time, if a club grew in numbers, then a small representative committee could be elected, when convenient.)

3. Club Room. The choice of somewhere to meet would obviously depend upon what places were available. It would be an advantage if a room or a hut could be found where a work-bench, materials, and tools could be kept; and where business and other meetings could be held.
4. Rules. These should be written in the minute book. The following are examples.

(*a*) That membership subscriptions be paid, weekly or as the club decides.

(*b*) That every member is expected to attend a meeting, when it is called.

(*c*) That resolutions be passed by a majority vote; and that in a case where there is an equal number of members voting for and against a resolution, then the chairman gives the casting vote, to decide whether the resolution be accepted or rejected.

(*d*) That all matters which concern the club be brought to a meeting for action to be taken.

(*e*) That such rules agreed upon may be added to when necessary; that a rule may be revised if the club think fit.

(*f*) That an annual general meeting be held. An outline of such a meeting is given below.

(*g*) That appointments be made and held on a yearly basis.

5. Club Activities. Suggestions for these are given in section 4 of this chapter.

6. Any Other Business (A.O.B. for short). Matters not previously dealt with would come under this heading.

7. Date, Time and Place of Next Meeting. The following items are offered for guidance at a further meeting: declare meeting open; read minutes of previous meeting, and sign them as a correct record; deal with any matters arising out of the minutes; deal with any further matters on the agenda, including a review of progress made, and any difficulties encountered; collect subscriptions; any other business; date and place of next meeting; declare the meeting closed.

Notes on Annual General Meeting

At this meeting appointments for the ensuing year would be made; and reports on the past year would be given, such as: first, the treasurer's audited statement, to be received by the meeting as being correct; second, the secretary's, on the number of meetings held during the year, average attendance and any other matters of interest; third, the leader's—a brief review of the year's activities, plus a comment upon the present state of the club. In addition to these reports, ideas and plans for the coming year could be suggested, discussed, and put to the vote.

Association of Kite Clubs

When a club has been formed in a new area, that club in turn should explore ways and means of starting another club. It will be realized that it takes time and experience for these things to work out. However, one may reasonably hope to see in due course, a local association being established.

In such an event, from the organization point of view, a president, secretary and treasurer would be needed, together with a number of representatives from each club. This body would be responsible for all inter-club activities. It is suggested that among other things, this committee could appoint a person to submit items of interest to the local press, and also could issue a magazine or bulletin.

An association committee might inquire into the possibilities of co-operating with other model and hobby clubs in the area, so that exchange visits could be arranged, joint exhibitions be held, and where possible, other joint activities be planned. There are great opportunities in kite-craft, if it be taken seriously, and dealt with enthusiastically.

ARRANGE ACTIVITIES

A club is defined as 'a group of persons possessing common or similar interests or occupations, who unite as an organized society' (*Universal English Dictionary*). But one's ideas of those interests should not be too narrow. Indeed, the aim of this book is to show kite-craft as a many-sided pastime. The focal point of attention, of course, is flying kites, but there are also opportunities for various activities within the framework of club life and organization. In making the most of these opportunities a club provides for the special aptitudes of the individual member, and it becomes a means of creative self-expression.

It follows from this then that a club, to be successful, must have a full and varied programme, which is carefully planned and carried through. The importance of this cannot be over-emphasized. It is a safeguard against the aimless, what-shall-we-do-next attitude which creeps in where there is no plan of action. And this is definitely not the way to progress.

Therefore a special meeting or meetings could be called for the specific purpose of discussing and planning a full and varied programme, covering a fixed period of say six or twelve months. As the club became established the matter could be dealt with at the annual general meeting, which at least might decide what things should be done, and also appoint members to get them done. Suggestions for various activities are now given and for the sake of convenience are listed under separate headings.

Club Kite Making

This could take place during the winter months or at any time when flying was not possible. The work could be done to a plan with regard to the number, sizes and styles of the kites. Chapters 1–6 will be a considerable help in this matter, and Chapter 9 may also be taken into account. Kites might be decorated with an emblem or a monogram—something simple, bold and finished in bright colours. For example, suppose the name was the Kingsford Kite Club. It could be called the 2-K Club, and a monogram—two K's intertwined—could be used as a distinguishing mark. The cost or part of the cost of all materials used by the members might be made a charge upon club funds. More will be said about the latter later.

Club Flights

These entail such matters as, first the choice of a site or base from which to fly the kites. Preliminary investigation would be needed in this respect, to find suitable and convenient places, which could be used in turn, and which could be marked on a base map, as described in Chapter 10.

Secondly, with regard to the actual flights, this may be said. Although it is recommended that these be planned in advance, and not carried out in a haphazard way, it is obvious that certain details such as cancellations or alterations of places, days and times would be attended to on a week by week basis.

Thirdly, at the start of a club's life, practice sessions would have an important place. By means of them, members could gain skill in handling different kites in varying weather conditions. And further, rehearsals could be held for the competitions which are suggested later in the chapter.

Exhibitions

It might seem at first that this is too ambitious a project where there are only a few members. In reply it must be said that enthusiasm is always more important than mere numbers. By planning well in advance it is often surprising how much the enthusiastic few can achieve.

In an exhibition, members' work, for example, may be shown. The many sizes and styles which are available in this book provide a means for staging a varied and interesting display. Another feature might be on the theme of kites through the ages (see 'Brief History', Chapter 12). This could be executed by means of posters briefly relating some of the interesting facts and figures which belong to the theme. Besides this, a large diagram might be drawn to illustrate how kites fly. Chapter 8 provides some useful information on this point.

Another suggestion deals with the weather factor in kite flying. The idea is to have on show large copies of the following: the Beaufort Scale, the list of main cloud types, a specimen weather map with explanatory notes on the symbols used, and perhaps a base map (see Chapter 10). This exhibit might also include a barometer, thermometer, compass and anemometer. (Instructions for making the two latter are given in Chapter 7.)

On the subject of exhibitions, a few general comments may be made. One is that on such an occasion refreshments could be provided and some form of entertainment given. In passing, these two, of course, might make a separate social evening. Another point is that an exhibition might be an inter-club venture, or a means of co-operating with other clubs, such as model glider or aeroplane. Lastly, an exhibition, if it were carefully planned and carried out, would do much to increase knowledge of and interest in one of the oldest pastimes in the world.

Open-air Displays

These are best staged on a large open site, which allows room for manoeuvres and for onlookers. But however good the site is, it is only a background for the displays. The most important thing is that the latter should be as effective as possible, and this is the intent of the following suggestions. They are entered under separate headings, to provide a means of quick reference.

(a) Moonlight Festival

The idea here is to stage a display of illuminated kites. These may be prepared in the following ways. Fasten an electric torch to each kite, over the centre of balance. A method of finding this is described in Chapter 8. Alternatively, a small dry battery may be used. Connect it to one or two bulbs by means of wires and a switch. In both cases it is suggested that coloured lights be used. Coloured transparent material can be placed round the torch glass or the bulbs.

In preparing the kites it must be remembered that they will be carrying extra weight. The additional equipment, therefore, should not be too heavy, and the larger-sized kites should be used. The box style is one of the most suitable for the purpose. As far as some other styles are concerned, very effective use could be made of transparent covers, made from a material like polythene.

On a suitable evening these multi-coloured lights, floating and weaving patterns overhead, would be a very pretty sight indeed. A further suggestion is that a camp-fire sing-song with refreshments might be included.

(b) Dual Control Display

Generally speaking, one line is used in flying a kite. In other words, it has a single control. The suggestion here is to incorporate a second line, attached to the bottom of the backbone. This line, of the same length as the kite line, would be suspended independent of a reel. By means of a dual control the operator could more readily manipulate his kite in an acrobatic display. One of the larger-sized kites would be needed to take up the extra weight, and only very light but strong lines should be used. Care would need to be taken with the second line, especially in coiling it round on the ground so that it would not get tangled during the flying of the kite. The main kite line would be used in sending the kite up; both lines could be used in bringing it down. This is an event which calls for considerable practice and skill

(c) Novelty Display

A striking effect would be ensured by flying kites of different styles, sizes and colours. The display would be enhanced by the addition on some of the kites of fringes, tassels, buzzers, multi-coloured tails, light reflecting and coloured discs. Instructions for making these are given in Chapter 7.

Competitions

These are divided into two classes: constructional and operational. Both provide fine opportunities for demonstrating skill in the making and flying of kites.

The first class is similar in many respects to the exhibition previously described, the difference being that the competitive element is now more in evidence. The entries are divided into groups, and awards are made for the following kites: the most original; the best-made; the most artistic; and the best kite in the show. The rule governing this competition is that all kites on show must have been flown satisfactorily.

The second class provides an opportunity for considering many interesting ideas and suggestions. The following are examples.

(a) Height and Speed Event

It should be said at the outset that kites can attain to great heights in the hands of experienced operators. But certain considerations have to be borne in mind. As a kite climbs higher it develops a stronger pull, and the pull of a large kite can be very strong indeed. Therefore, in a contest of this kind, the young beginner should not be tempted to fly too large a kite at too great a height.

Because height is one of the governing factors in this event, the competitors' kite lines must be of equal length. The lines also incorporate a simple device for measuring heights. Small bands of coloured thread are tied to them at fixed distances, say 5 ft. or 10 ft. As a line is being wound in, it is a simple matter to count the bands and to multiply their number by the distance each represents. Speed is the other factor, and so a time-limit is laid down. This could be decided in a preliminary practice. Independent timekeepers and line checkers are needed.

At the signal to start the competitors launch their kites. The winner is the one who succeeds in flying his to the limit of its line in the shortest time. If no one manages to do this in the time which is set, then the one who comes nearest to it gains the first place. This entails measuring the kite lines, and this is done by the checkers, who are then able to declared the winner.

The rule governing the event is that the kites must be brought as far as possible to an overhead position. Any kite moving off downwind no matter how much line has been paid out is disqualified.

(b) Formation Event

For this, members make up small teams, each under a leader. At the signal to start they launch their kites and after climbing for a while endeavour to move in formation. Any team whose kites touch one another, or stray too obviously out of line, receive a point against, and not merely once, but every time such an incident occurs. The aim is to keep the kites in each team from start to finish as close as possible to one another without actually touching. At the end of a given time points against are added up, and the winning team declared. This event calls for combined skill, and much also depends upon the leader. A checker is needed for each team. He records any points made against his team. These are examined and compared by a referee, who has also been keeping a close watch on the proceedings, and he announces the winning team.

(c) Landing in a Target Area

The target area is a marked-out square which is plainly seen by the competitors, but is some distance away from them. Every competitor in turn brings his kite to an overhead position and then, not moving past a touch line, tries to land his kite in the target area. If no kite is brought down in the area, then the one nearest to it is awarded first place. If more than one kite lands in the area, then the one nearest to the centre is the winner.

A referee is needed to measure where the kites land in relation to the target area. In addition, a checker stands by the touch line to see that no competitor goes past it. If he does, then he is disqualified. Like the previous event, this is suitable for team entries. But whether the kites are flown by members on their own or in teams they have to be handled with some skill and judgement.

(d) Parachute Recovery

The method of making and releasing parachutes is described in Chapter 7. Each competitor receives an equal number of parachutes, say six. Each competitor's parachutes are a different colour from the others, so that they can be easily identified. At the signal to start, the parachutes are sent up, released and recovered as quickly as possible. One assistant works with each competitor. If no one succeeds in finding all his parachutes in a fixed time, then the one who comes next best is the winner. In the case of a tie, the procedure is repeated by the two competitors to find the winning one.

(e) Balloon Release

This is a variation of the above event. The method of attaching the balloons to the kite lines is the same as for the parachutes, namely, by means of hooks and strings.

(f) Balloon Bursting

Here is a contest which bears a resemblance to the old Chinese sport of kite fighting. In the latter the kite lines were coated at the top with glue and glass fragments, and each competitor tried to cut his opponent's line. In the balloon contest one or two fine nails project from each kite. Competitors send up a given number of balloons on their lines, to which they are attached by strings of varying lengths. The aim is for each of two contestants to burst as many of his opponent's balloons as he can in a given time.

(g) Buried Treasure

A hunt for buried treasure is always a popular game, and this one will arouse a great deal of interest. The organizer hides a small box containing the treasure or prize. Maps are drawn on small pieces of paper, which give clues to the whereabouts of the treasure. Blank pieces of paper, the same size as the maps, and parachutes in different colours for each competitor, are also required.

Two out of a total number of six parachutes for each contestant have maps attached to them, the rest are blanks. The organizer is the one who prepares the parachutes for the hunt. At the signal to start, the parachutes are sent up the kite lines and released. Each competitor has to release all his parachutes before he can begin the hunt. With the help of an assistant he tries to find one of his own maps and not one belonging to another. If one is found, then it has to be decoded, so as to lead to the buried treasure. At the end of a given time, if the treasure has not been found, then the contestants may say where they think it might be hidden. The one whose guess comes nearest to the actual spot is the winner.

Further Suggestions for Competitions

Competitions might be arranged as an inter-club venture, and organized on the basis of heats, semi-finals and finals. But in both cases of members of one club or of competing clubs, some scheme of awards might be considered, these being held for a period of twelve months.

One suggestion is that an award could take the form of a small shield or a framed certificate. A local craftsman or a club member might be able to make a small wooden shield. On this a few suitable words could be neatly painted. An inscription in gold or silver paint upon a red or blue background would look very effective. As an alternative a framed certificate might be executed after the style of an illuminated manuscript. An example of a shield is given in Chapter 7. This suggestion also covers second and third place awards, these possibly being in the form of smaller framed certificates.

A further suggestion is that the awards might be presented at a special meeting. If this were agreed, then the following matters could be decided: who should be invited to present the awards; where the meeting could be held, and what other items could be planned, to help to make it an enjoyable occasion.

In passing, the practice of making awards is to be commended, because it provides a goal for competitive endeavour. And in the atmosphere of friendly rivalry a club may flourish.

SUGGESTIONS FOR OTHER ACTIVITIES

(a) Club Magazine

A small magazine, printed on a duplicator could be an interesting and successful project. It could be published once a quarter or even annually. One way of meeting the cost of production would be to make it a charge upon club funds.

The following is a suggested layout: news and drawings of club activities, outdoor and indoor; kite topics in general; review of the weather; outside contributions on the subject of other hobbies, including perhaps model gliders and aeroplanes. These subjects, together with any others accepted by the editor, would provide sufficient material for an interesting magazine. All that remains to be said is that it should be well-designed and neatly printed; and that every member should try to make it known to and read by others.

(b) Club Weather Station

This suggestion arises out of what has been written in Chapter 10 on the subject of the weather. An amateur station could be set up at home or at club headquarters. In the latter case members might make up a rota by means of which daily notes could be taken of temperature; pressure; cloud formation; wind direction and speed. In this way weather trends could be studied, and estimates of coming flying conditions could be attempted. A kite club weather station would probably arouse considerable local interest, for everyone is interested in the weather. This in itself would help to keep the fact of the club's existence in people's minds. Of course, the project, if attempted, does require that one member at least should be well-informed on the subject.

Talks, Discussions and Outings

In a balanced club programme talks and discussions are given a place. The following are a few of the subjects which could be considered. The first is the story of kites through the ages, as outlined in the brief history in Chapter 12. The second is on popularizing kite flying. The third deals with the theme of how kites fly (see Chapter 8). Again, if there were any speakers available who were interested in other hobbies, such as model gliders or aeroplanes, then they could be invited to give a talk.

In a general sense, club outings could be in the form of visits to places of historic or other interest. Other outings could have a particular reference to kite flying. For example, one might be organized as a survey of one's area, in order to discover suitable flying bases. Another might be for the purpose of noting the physical characteristics of the area, in order to discover whether these had any bearing upon local weather.

Kites and the Camera

The suggestion here is that a camera might be part of a club's equipment. On many occasions photographs could be taken in order to build up a pictorial record of activities, such as exhibitions; displays; competitions; outings and the like. In time, a club album would be a much-prized possession.

Club Funds

In running a club some expense is incurred by materials, heating and lighting, magazine production, stationery, and so on. Apart from membership subscriptions, other sources of income might be found in some activities where charges could be made for admittance and refreshments. In addition, there may be interested people who would respond to an appeal on behalf of such funds. And if a magazine were published, then a small charge might be made for the copies.

CHAPTER TWELVE

A brief history of kites

KITE flying is one of the oldest pastimes in the world. No one can say with certainty precisely how old it is, but we do know that it goes back for many centuries, and that the beginnings of the story have an eastern setting. On the latter point, more will be said in a moment. In the meantime, this may be said. In its general significance, the invention of the kite stands out as an expression of man's age-old and universal longing to conquer the air.

It cannot be said with precision just how or when thoughts about flying began to occupy man's mind. What is known, however, is that from the time he began to write and to draw, the idea of flight was present; an idea which was born, no doubt, through watching the birds in their travels, doing what he himself could not do. The ability which he himself did not possess he bestowed upon the beings born of his imagination. In ancient stories of superhuman mastery of the elements, gods and devils transport themselves with wings, and men and beasts also navigate the air. Thus in one way or another man's interest in flight was sustained, and in the course of time this interest led to various attempts to achieve mastery of the air.

In the story of man's conquest of the air, kites have an important place. It cannot be said with certainty who invented them or when they were first flown. Ancient Greek tradition ascribes the invention to Archytas of Tarentum in the fourth century B.C. The Koreans attribute the origin of the kite to a general who, in the dim and distant past, put fresh courage into his troops by sending up a kite to which a lantern was fixed. They believed that it was a new star and a sign of divine help.

Above the mists of speculation the fourth century B.C. stands as a landmark. It is established that by this time kites were well-known in China. It is said that the first Chinese kites were probably made of wood. This could well be, though a case could be made out that they might have had a bamboo framework with a silk cover, since silk is said to have been used there as far back as 4,000 years ago. It is probable that by the fourth century this material was being used. About the year A.D. 105 the Chinese discovered a method of making paper sheets from vegetable fibre. This made available another suitable covering material.

When we turn to the purposes for which kites were used in those far-off days, much that is of interest may be noted. Ancient Chinese historians have recorded that they were employed to carry ropes across rivers and gorges. The ropes were made fast, and wooden bridges suspended from them. It is said that a general of the Han dynasty (206 B.C.–A.D. 221) put the enemy to flight by flying musical kites over their camp at night. The enemy fled, because they believed that the music was the voices of their guardian angels, warning them of coming danger. There is a tradition, too, that man-lifting kites were used in attacks on cities, and to drop men behind enemy lines. It is difficult to say when this strategy was first employed, so no date can be given. It is known, however, that the Chinese and the Japanese used man-lifting kites to survey the enemy's position as early as the seventeenth century A.D.

We now consider kite flying as a national pastime in China. By the early centuries A.D. kites were being made in a great variety of shapes, representing, for example, men, birds, animals and monsters. There were kites which carried lanterns, strings, pipes and small windmills. (In the latter perhaps there is the germ of an idea for an aircraft propeller.) Again, some were adapted for the sport of kite-fighting. The upper parts of the control lines were coated with glue and ground glass. It was the aim of a competitor to cut his opponent's line and bring his kite down.

Scenes which presented a variety of colour, form, and movement were displayed through the centuries. One author, some years ago, described such a scene, wherein the sky would be full of all sorts of kites, which were being flown by old and young alike. A personal recollection of this fondness for kite flying may not be out of place here. Not so long ago, the writer saw two elderly Chinese, skilfully flying their kites in the grounds of a certain hospital, while other patients who were fit enough, were playing cricket, or otherwise passing the time. (An illustration of Chinese flying kites will be seen in Plate V.)

There is a tradition that kites were known in Ancient Greece and Rome. One should not be too dogmatic on this point. On the other hand, taking fourth century China as the starting point, one may confidently trace the spread of kite flying all over Asia and beyond, extending to such countries as New Zealand. The Maoris are said to have fastened perforated reeds to their kites. It was believed that the sounds which they made would scare off evil spirits.

Kite flying was established in Europe by the fifteenth century. It may well have been known for some time before this, possibly being introduced by voyagers to the east. Marco Polo, the traveller from Venice, arrived in China at the close of the thirteenth century. He stayed there for seventeen years. During this time he became a member of the Emperor's staff and moved freely about the country. When he returned to Venice with a valuable collection of things, people would not believe the stories he told. One is tempted to think that a kite found a place among the things which he brought back. At any rate, as he talked of the people and places he had seen, it is possible that he did mention their fondness for kite flying. In the search for the origin of the kite in Europe, there must also be borne in mind the possibility that they were brought in as occasional novelties by traders with the east.

We move now from the realm of might-have-been to that of certainty. In the year 1405 illustrations of hot-air kites are shown in German manuscripts. They were a cross between a kite and a balloon. They were dragon-shaped and hollow and had a light inside them. Apparently they were used as military standards, and were flown by means of cords held by horsemen. The diamond-shaped kite made its appearance in Europe in the sixteenth century, and from the evidence which can be gathered it seems that this remained the basic shape for a long time. An illustration in John Bate's *Mysteries of Nature and Art*, published in 1635, shows one of these kites with a bridle and a tail rather longer than the kite itself.

In the course of kite history we follow a path which brings us eventually to the invention of the aeroplane. Every invention must have an inventor, and in the history of the aeroplane Sir George Cayley has an important place. He has been called the true inventor of the aeroplane. He lived and carried out most of his research work at Brompton Hall, near Scarborough in Yorkshire. He was a man with an inquiring mind, and in his search for the principles governing flight he made repeated tests with

paper and kites. He came to realize what is called the aero-
dynamic significance of the kite. He applied his knowledge in
such a way that the aeroplane eventually became a reality and
not just a dream. It may be realized how important apparently
simple experiments can be when it is remembered that on the
basis of his experiments he was able to lay down the scientific
principles of heavier-than-air flight. He observed his kites as they
moved in the air, his inquiring mind probing into the secret of
their flight. How much is owed by the world of today to this
great man, experimenting with simple objects which contained a
wonderful promise of the shape of things to come!

It is interesting to read Cayley's own words about his experiments with kites. In 1804 he wrote: 'A common paper kite containing 154 square inches was fastened to a rod of wood at the
hinder end, and supported from the front part from the same
rod by a peg, so as to make an angle of 6°. With it this rod pro-
ceeded on behind the kite and supported a tail, made of two
planes crossing each other at right angles, containing 20 inches
each. This tail could be set to any angle with the stick. The centre
of gravity was varied by sticking a weight with a sharp point into
the stick. If a velocity of 15 feet per second was given to it in an
horizontal direction, it would skim for 20 or 30 yards supporting
its own weight, and if pointed downward in an angle of about
18°, it would proceed uniformly in a right line for ever with a
velocity of 15 feet per second. It was very pretty to see it sail down
a steep hill, and it gave the idea that a larger instrument would be
a better and a safer conveyance down the Alps than even the sure-
footed mule. . . . The least inclination of the tail towards the right
or left made it shape its course like a ship by the rudder.' (An
illustration of this kite-glider will be seen in Plate VII.)

The above words, it has been said, are a description of the
world's first true aeroplane. The machine had a pegtop kite for
the wing, which was attached to a pole at an angle of 6 degrees
from the horizontal. The kite-like tail had two pieces, set at right
angles to each other. In later machines which he built and flew,
the kite-cum-glider look was preserved. Some were flown by
means of a towing rope; free flights were made by others, in
which passengers were carried. The story goes that somewhat
reluctantly, Sir George's coachman made a flight in one of the
machines. He was dragged across a valley and came down with

a crash. Picking himself up out of the wreckage, he stumbled to his master and said he was giving up his job, because he had been hired to drive and not to fly. However, it is through men like Cayley, and it may be added, his coachman, that progress is made.

Another air-minded gentleman, George Pocock, deserves a place in the history of the kite. In 1825, one of his kites made an ascent, carrying up his daughter Martha. She was one of the first women to fly. One wonders how she felt during this short pioneering flight. She must have had great confidence in her father and his man-carrying kite. In 1827 he published a work entitled *The Aeropleustic Art or Navigation in the Air by the Use of Kites or Buoyant Sails*. In the same year he harnessed two very large kites to a carriage. He tested this kite-carriage on the public highway and travelled some distance between Bristol and Marlborough. It is recorded that he easily overtook the London mail coach en route. The sight of a carriage bowling along without horses must have caused some alarm, wonder and amusement among the onlookers. And no doubt the thrifty-minded hailed it as a very cheap means of transport.

In 1859 E. J. Cordner, an Irish Catholic priest, invented a man-lifting kite apparatus for ship-to-shore rescue work. A number of kites were used to lift a single-passenger car from the ship and to convey it to the shore. Although the system was tested it was not used in actual rescue work. Such work as this was hindered because of the old superstition that anyone who rescued another from the sea, would himself be drowned within the year.

From the sea and ships we return to the air and aircraft. Experiments and developments continued to show the influence of the kite, and particularly this is the case with the box kite. Any reference to the box kite in a historical context must be linked to a name famous in kite history, that of Lawrence Hargrave (or Hargreave). In 1884 this Australian began his experiments which resulted in the invention of the box kite in 1893. This invention was greeted with enthusiasm on both sides of the Atlantic within the space of a few months. Such a reception is not hard to understand, because the box kite has proved itself to be superior in lift and stability. The most popular form of Hargrave's kites consisted of two large oblong cloth boxes, open on two sides and secured to a framework. An illustration of the kite will be seen in Plate IV.

Hargrave came to England in 1899. His lectures and demonstrations did much to popularize his kites which were already familiar to aircraft pioneers.

Whilst he was in England Hargrave lent some of his kites to P. S. Pilcher, who wished to test them in his experiments in the direction of powered flight. Pilcher, a well-known glider pilot, designed an aircraft, which presumably showed the influence of the box-kite in its structure, and which he intended to demonstrate. Unfortunately he was seriously injured when another of his aircraft, the Hawk, crashed during an experimental flight, and he died soon afterwards. Hargrave himself had an idea, which apparently was not followed up, of linking a number of his kites together, and suspending an engine and a propeller from them. He thought that when the cable anchor was freed the machine would continue under its own power.

In continuing the story, a brief account may be given of the achievements of other pioneers. Captain B. F. S. Baden-Powell, brother of the founder of the Scout movement, was one of them. He was a well-known balloonist, who at Pirbright Camp in 1894, successfully demonstrated his man-lifting kites. A few years later, H. D. Wise tried out a linked series of box-kites which were able to lift a man.

In this brief list of pioneers a special place must be given to Samuel Franklin Cody. He was born in America, and became a naturalized Englishman in 1896. One biography states that he was the first man to fly in Great Britain, and was the maker of the first practical British flying machine. Cody worked at the War Office Kite and Balloon Factory at Farnborough. He patented his man-lifting kites in 1901. They followed the pattern set by Baden-Powell, that is, in the form of a train or linked series. Cody's kite system was officially adopted by the War Office in 1904. In this system the operator was carried by one kite, which was connected to the other kites by means of a cable. The carrier-kite could be raised or lowered on the cable. It appears that there were also cords by means of which the operator could make the carrier-kite swivel to the right or the left. It is interesting to note that Mrs Cody, following Martha Pocock's example, made a few ascents with her husband's kites. In 1903, Cody made a Channel crossing from France to England. This he accomplished in a specially made boat which was harnessed to a kite

—hence the name, kite-boat. He also fitted an engine to a modified kite, called a power-kite, and in it he made what is called the first short aeroplane flight in England.

The link between the kite and the aeroplane is stressed in a statement made by O. L. Owen, a writer on aviation. He says: 'All the successful gliders and power-driven planes of the experimental period were based to a large extent upon the principles of the box-kite.' We may also note what another authority on the subject, C. H. Gibbs-Smith, says: 'The first successful biplanes in Europe (1905–10) were not only based on these kites, but were colloquially referred to as "box-kites".'

Space is too limited to allow more than a brief mention of that daring and resourceful aviator, Octave Chanute. He was an American who designed and experimented with many machines and made over 1,000 flights. One illustration depicts him as literally hanging on in the air to a craft which had box-kite type wings and a kite-like tail.

His fellow-countrymen, Wilbur and Orville Wright, won never-dying fame in the world of flight. They were the sons of a bishop and lived at Dayton, Ohio. An early interest in kites was the starting point on the road which led to great achievements. In September 1900, they took their first glider to the sand dunes of Kitty Hawk, on the coast of North Carolina. The machine was mostly flown as a kite, being controlled by cords reaching to the ground. On one or two occasions it was flown as a glider, and some successful flights were made. These were the signs and promises of greater things to come.

From America we turn to Europe and to Alberto Santos-Dumont, a wealthy Brazilian who lived in France. He borrowed Hargrave's box-kite idea, and built a machine which was virtually a box-kite plus an engine. At Bagatelle, near Paris, in 1906, he won the French Aero Club's prize for the first public aeroplane flight in Europe by flying 25 metres.

In passing, the influence of the box-kite in aeroplane design of this period is shown in the illustration of the Voisin biplane (see Plate I.)

Another style of kite makes an appearance at this time, and it is associated with the name of Dr Alexander Graham Bell, who is known as the inventor of the first practical telephone in 1876. He designed a tetrahedral kite, which as the name implies was a triangular pyramid. It was tried out first as a man-lifting kite and then in 1909 an engine and propeller were fitted. The machine just managed to lift a man into the air and the idea was dropped.

Through the 'nineties and into the dawn of the twentieth century, enthusiasts in various parts of the world were making hazardous experiments with kites and kite-like machines. They were persistent and courageous in their attempts to conquer the air. By their devotion to a great idea they blazed a trail which leads to the aeroplane of today.

Passengers in the great flying machines of the modern world owe a great debt to the kite and to those who realized and worked out its inherent possibilities. It may not be easy at first to discern any connexion between the kite and the aeroplane. It is to be hoped that this brief history will make this connexion a little more obvious, and will help the reader to understand what Captain Ferber meant when he declared that the kite was only an anchored aeroplane. It is true that he was referring to the aeroplanes of his own day, that is to say, the experimental period which has been under review. During this time many of the machines, as we have seen, showed the influence of the kite very plainly in their design. As a result of this likeness between the two, people then may indeed have regarded the kite as an anchored aeroplane, and to put it the other way round, the aeroplane as an unanchored kite. But the meaning of Ferber's statement goes deeper than a passing likeness. In other words, the statement says that the forces which operate in flying a kite also operate in the flight of an aeroplane. Therefore, though the aeroplane of today may, in some respects, seem far removed from the earlier machines, and even farther from the kite, the connexion between the kite and the aeroplane remains. In flight both are subject to the influence of resistance; propulsion; lift and weight.

In the course of its history the kite has been linked to other great names and events. In order to show this, the eighteenth century is taken for the starting point. In 1706 Benjamin Franklin was born in Boston, Massachusetts. This great American states-man was an authority on meteorology. In 1746 he began to study the problems of electricity. In 1752 he carried out a demonstration to prove that lightning is electrical energy. He flew a kite in a thunderstorm in order to draw electricity from the clouds. He fastened a key to the kite wire-line, to which he also attached a silk ribbon. The ribbon was to prevent the lightning from passing through his body. The lightning travelled down the line and was conducted to earth. When he announced to the Royal Society that his kite had drawn lightning from the clouds, he was laughed at; but later it had to be admitted that what he said was true. As a result of his experiment, he invented his lightning conductor in 1753. When it is recorded that the Empire State Building in New York was struck by lightning sixty-three times in three years it proves the importance of efficient conductors, and therefore proves the importance of Franklin's discovery. It is interesting to note that a kite played a part in the invention of this safety device. Incidentally, when he was a boy, Franklin used a kite to draw him across a lake when bathing. He declared that the English Channel could be crossed by the same means.

Franklin's demonstration with a kite is but one instance of their being used in connexion with the weather. The weather is a subject of never-failing interest, therefore it is worth noting that to help people to know more about it, the kite has played an important part. In the nineteenth century, kites began to be used to carry meteorological instruments and this practice continued to well into the present century. An outstanding ascent by meteorological kites took place in Germany, in 1905. The foremost of a train of six attained a height of four miles. This ascent was over half-way through the troposphere—the lowest layer of the atmosphere; and it provided valuable information about temperature, pressure and humidity at high altitudes.

Guglielmo Marconi, like Benjamin Franklin, was deeply interested in electricity. This interest was obvious even when he was a small boy. In 1895, he started to experiment with methods of sending and receiving the electrical impulses, called Hertzian waves. This was a stage in the progress towards that day, 12th December, 1901, when he picked up the first wireless signals to be sent across the Atlantic Ocean, from Poldhu in Cornwall to St John's, Newfoundland. The name of this wireless pioneer is known universally, what is not so widely known is that his great achievement in 1901 was accomplished with the aid of a kite. Marconi used it to support an aerial, outside the barracks of St John's, where he had installed his apparatus.

During World War I (1914–18) kites did service to the armed forces in the form of kite-balloons. A tail of kites was attached to the balloon to keep it steady. Kite-balloons were used in aerial observation, and attained an operational height of about 5,000 feet. They were also flown at sea by ships protecting convoys, to keep a watch for German submarines. In addition, kite-balloons were employed in Britain as a form of air defence. This was achieved by making them support nets of thin steel cables to foul enemy aircraft. In World War II (1939–45) kites continued to give valuable service. They were used after the manner of Marconi's kite, to support wireless aerials. They were sent up from boats and rafts by survivors from wrecked ships or planes.

This brief history would be incomplete without some reference to the name, kite. The original form and meaning of the word are doubtful. The present form of the word goes back to the Middle English period of the English language (A.D. 1100–1500). As to its meaning, in the first place, we know that it is the name given to a bird of prey, a member of the falcon family, and of the order of the hawks. Secondly, as the word hawk in this connexion means 'to seize', thus denoting a characteristic of these birds, so etymologically, the name kite would seem to denote the graceful soaring flight of the birds of this name. Gilbert White in *The Natural History of Selborne* describes this flight in these words: 'Thus kites . . . sail round in circles with wings expanded and motionless.' Thirdly, the traditional diamond-shaped kite, when it is high in the air, bears some resemblance to this bird of prey. Thus one may visualize how our forefathers might have come to apply the name to a man-made contrivance, for in both cases soaring flight is an important feature.

We have looked back upon the kite's participation in some of the notable achievements of the past. We have taken, as it were, a 'kite's-eye' view of people, places and events. This survey has covered many centuries and countries, so that it may truly be said that the kite, from the historical point of view, has an international significance.

As far as the prospects of kite flying are concerned, we believe that it will long continue to be an interesting and rewarding pastime all over the world.

CHAPTER THIRTEEN

The educational value of kite-craft

THE aim of this book is to show that kites, besides having a healthy open-air appeal, have an instructive value. A few things may be said therefore about the educational aspects of the hobby, in the hope that what is said may prove to be helpful to those who have not regarded the hobby from this point of view.

Making a kite is an activity which develops skill. However simple it might be, a kite must be properly made, if it is to fly. A kite is sometimes described as a toy, and this may be misleading, in that it might obscure the idea that a kite must conform to certain principles, otherwise it will be a failure. In the broad sense of the word a kite is an aircraft and not merely a toy. When this is understood and applied then it becomes apparent that the making of a kite certainly encourages and develops skill.

Kite making appeals to the imagination. In this respect there is a freedom of choice which is particularly attractive. It encourages experiments in design, to which fact the diverse shapes of kites testify. It provides opportunities for pictorial expression, by means of the emblems and patterns with which they may be decorated.

Making a kite is a project in which every part is significant and related to certain principles—the principles governing the flight of heavier-than-air craft. A rough piece of wood may serve as a crude boat. Basically, it can do what the most modern and luxurious liner can do: float upon the water and move along. But in the air things are different. Any rough and ready structure will not fly. Although something may be made which bears a resemblance to a kite or an aeroplane it will be incapable of flight if it transgresses the principles of flight. This very fact brings us to another point which is worth considering.

Kite making and flying, serve as an introduction to aerodynamics. This is defined as that branch of physics which deals with the forces which act on bodies moving through the air. A

151

shorter definition is that it is the science of flight. In an air-minded age, this is obviously a subject of importance. Although aerodynamics, in its advanced stages, is the province of the specialist, it does not rule out the suggestion that the elementary stages have their place in modern general education. Kite flying offers a means of grasping the rudiments of the subject.

Again, kite flying may serve as an introduction to meteorology, for the weather and kite flying are closely related. This relationship is dealt with in Chapter 10. All that needs to be done here is to underline the connexion between the two and further to suggest that the study of the weather, apart from being of importance in itself, may be linked to local geographical and nature studies. This suggestion is offered in the belief that knowledge of the local natural features helps towards an understanding of the wider content of a subject such as meteorology.

One other point is that kite making and flying may become a corporate venture, expressed in the aims and activities of a club. As such it provides opportunities for participation in discussions, planning and organization, which may develop the sometimes unsuspected abilities of the individual member.

It is to be hoped that this chapter, in some measure, has served to show that kites have a definite, though not too obtrusive, educational aspect. This being so, their possibilities in the realm of instruction deserve to be explored to the fullest extent both for the pleasure and the profit they may bring.

Index